GrATTITUDE

Other Books by Ace Collins

9-3-19

GrATTITUDE

PRACTICING CONTAGIOUS OPTIMISM
FOR POSITIVE CHANGE

ACE COLLINS

ZONDERVAN.com/
AUTHORTRACKER
follow your favorite authors

ZONDERVAN

Grattitude
Copyright © 2010 by Andrew Collins

This title is also available as a Zondervan ebook.
Visitwww.zondervan.com/ebooks.

This title is also available in a Zondervan audio edition.
Visit www.zondervan.fm.

Requests for information should be addressed to:

Zondervan, *Grand Rapids, Michigan 49530*

Library of Congress Cataloging-in-Publication Data

Collins, Ace.
     Gratitude : practicing contagious optimism for positive change / Ace
  Collins.
       p.   cm.
    Includes bibliographical references.
    ISBN 978-0-310-32477-5 (softcover)
     1. Attitude change—Religious aspects—Christianity. 2. Attitude
  (Psychology)—Religious aspects—Christianity. 3. Christian life. I. Title.
  II. Title: Gratitude.
  BV4597.2 M65—2010
  241'.4—dc22
                        2010005333

Any Internet addresses (websites, blogs, etc.) and telephone numbers printed in this book are offered as a resource. They are not intended in any way to be or imply an endorsement by Zondervan, nor does Zondervan vouch for the content of these sites and numbers for the life of this book.

Interior design: Michael Lautenbach

Printed in the United States of America

---

10 11 12 13 14 /DCI/ 20 19 18 17 16 15 14 13 12 11 10 9 8 7 6 5 4 3 2 1

To Gayla,
who seems always to find the sunshine,
even on cloudy days

CONTENTS

Introduction

Discovering the Power of Grattitude

We all know at least one amazing person who, no matter what tragedy or trauma he or she may be facing, seems to maintain a contagious optimism. Looking at such strength of character and graciousness, even in the midst of storms, we can't help but feel inspired.

For me, that person is Janie. We attended the same high school, and Janie always had a knack for making people laugh. When I reconnected with her twenty years after graduation, I was saddened to learn that Janie had gone blind.

Janie's childhood diabetes had taken a great deal more than her sight. When she went blind, her husband divorced her, and he won custody of her two greatest treasures — her sons. Though she was in her early thirties, her kidneys were already beginning to fail.

Now, years later, even as she faces additional health challenges, sparkling hope still fills her sightless blue eyes. She is enjoying life more than ever. No bitterness infects Janie's tone when she speaks of what she has lost. Rather than dwelling on the pain and darkness that now dominated her world, she is working on her college degree and experiencing the excitement of feeling her way through her new world.

Janie is amazing. Even though she has every right to be bitter, Janie still believes her life is filled with wonder, newness, and joy.

What is her secret?

We can meet smiling, optimistic people in prisons, cancer wards, nursing homes, and on the street. Why are some people happy while others, who have far more, are depressed?

It isn't what such people *have* but what they *don't* have. People like Janie have thrown away the junk that fills the minds of so many of us. Their minds are lean, efficient machines that run on optimism and hope.

We too can open up our minds to optimism. By losing some of the heavy, negative things that we have chained inside our heads, we can gain a world of hope. Like Janie, we can learn to embrace happiness for ourselves and to share it with others. Let's discover what we have to be grateful for and let our souls fly.

When times are tough, we want directions. Our map for attitude change comes from looking at those around us whom we admire and respect. By using our heroes as inspirational role models, we will have a much better reason to stay the course. We can use their proven attitudes — what we'll learn to call *grattitudes* — as a map to our goals. As we study how our heroes handle each of life's great challenges, we will learn how to embrace our own blessings.

There is an old gospel song called "Keep on the Sunny

Side." Grattitudes do not hide in the darkness but are found on the sunny side of life's road. When we have a positive attitude, we foster an environment where we are ready to see good in almost every situation. With grattitudes, our attitudes are not covered by clouds but are open to see the sunshine. When we walk on the sunny side of life, we are much happier and more productive. But how do we get there? How do we get past the trash that fills so much of our world and find an opening to really see our blessings?

Before we can have real grattitudes, we need to lose our mental garbage. In these pages, we will examine the spiritual price of isolation, pride, and prejudice and discover how they spawn misery and pain. Then we will learn how to get rid of the attitudes that hold us back, and replace them with something better. A life whose driving force is gratitude is a life that can survive almost anything.

Janie saw the world as a place filled with potential, and she never let self-pity blind her to all the opportunities to be a friend to others. One night at choir practice, one of the members said to the smiling Janie, "You're my hero." Janie tilted her head to the side and grinned, sincerely asking, "Why?"

Before the person could explain, Janie answered the question through her actions. Turning, she said to another member of the choir, "I heard your husband is sick—is there something I can do for you? Is there anything you need?" Janie, who had been in and out of the hospital sixteen times in two years, battling diabetes, wasn't dwelling on her problems. Rather she was trying to lift the load from someone else's shoulders.

Janie understands grattitudes, and by the time this book is finished, I hope you will too.

One of the best ways to begin changing our mental habits is to acknowledge positive qualities that we admire in other people and ask how we can apply them to our lives. Our goal should be to take the best grattitudes we know and make them our own.

So right now, before reading the main part of the book, here is a challenge: Make a list of the ten people you most admire. Beside each person's name, write their strongest character trait. This is their grattitude quality.

Next, expand the list to include something concrete you can do in your life to emulate each person's grattitude quality. Be practical. What is something you can do today or in the next few days to reflect their attitude and behavior in your own life?

Whenever possible, let the individuals know that they inspire you. Sharing this will demonstrate to them that they are making a meaningful impact in the lives of others. This will encourage *them* to continue to spread their grattitudes, and it will motivate *you* to keep on keeping on, since you know your hero is watching.

Now that your list is written, let me share mine with you. These are the ten grattitudes I believe are vital to living a productive, happy, and meaningful life.

GRATTITUDE 1

SELF-DISCIPLINE

Self-discipline is one of life's most vital grattitudes. It is what we need to push us all the way to our goals, and not merely partway. The mountain climber doesn't quit until he is standing on the peak, where he forgets the struggle and danger of the climb. The marathoner pushes through the wall at the twenty-mile mark. The writer works until she can write, "The End." Disciplined individuals don't sacrifice their principles or cut corners when pursuing a goal. They finish the job and do it right. And because of their self-discipline, they don't just reach their potential; they exceed it!

Barbara Mandrell is a now legendary name in the world of entertainment, but she was just another up-and-coming wannabe when I saw her onstage for the first time in 1975. At that point, she had only two Top 10 records and no signature hits. When I purchased the ticket to that show, I wanted to see the headline act — the Statler Brothers. Yet within ten minutes of Barbara taking the stage as the opening act, I was blown away. I had never seen a performer as skilled as this tiny blonde. I expected her to sing, and she did that well, but she did so much more. She played every instrument on the stage and performed with such incredible energy, I came to the conclusion that she must have swallowed a tornado, because she was a whirlwind of rare energy. I told my new bride, "Can you imagine how long it took to refine those skills and develop this show?" I may not have known much about Barbara when I walked into the auditorium, but she had my admiration and respect when I walked out. I also couldn't wait to see her work again.

That first night I caught Barbara, she was just one of a score of pretty new faces with good voices trying to make their mark in country music, but within three years, while the others had faded into the background, she would be the defining image for an entire industry. How could someone who was still in her twenties emerge as one of the most consummate entertainers in the history of show business? Well, I can guarantee you this: luck had nothing to do with it. Barbara stood out as something new and fresh because she embraced self-discipline.

More than most people I have known, Barbara Mandrell fully understood the price of reaching her goal, and she had the self-discipline to get her there. The spark was born as she took full advantage of her parents' music store in the community of Oceanside, California. As a girl, Barbara met several well-known performers who came into the Mandrell store to purchase supplies. She listened to their stories and began to understand how much joy they received through the art of entertainment. Their tales of spotlights and stage thrilled her. She also heard these men and women talk about their hours and hours in recording studios and years spent honing their skills. Other kids might have taken these stories and been inspired to spend a few months in music lessons, but for most the practice time would have eventually tempered their dreams of fame. Yet for Barbara, who was already focused on winning every race on the playground and every contest in school, the price wasn't too scary. Even as a preteen, she saw the big picture.

Seeing the big picture is essentially the beginning of being self-disciplined and is what keeps you focused on the daily work of improving your skills. What makes one able to reach one's goal is coming to the full understanding that the little daily steps that must be taken. In Barbara's case, these small steps consisted of learning something new each day on a musical instrument. It might have been as simple as a riff, chord, or song, but moving forward each day, accomplishing small goals, was vital to reaching the big goal. So while others her age spent hours with their dolls or toys, day by day and step by step, over several years, Barbara learned how to play everything from the accordion to the steel guitar. And she just didn't learn a song or two; she drove herself to master each of those instruments.

The practice paid off, and by junior high Barbara was

wowing audiences up and down the West Coast while appearing on shows that starred the icons of the age, including Red Foley and Johnny Cash. She was even featured on a West Coast television show. Fans recognized her talent, but musicians were amazed at her desire to push forward, to learn more, and to spend long hours practicing.

Self-discipline is often derailed by roadblocks, which can create insecurity, frustration, and fear. In Barbara's case, the giant roadblock landed in her path when she was just fourteen. She had been working a series of dates with country music legend Patsy Cline, who had become a second mother to her. The young performer idolized the superstar singer. After a show in Kansas City, Barbara left the tour to go back home with her parents. At about the same time, Patsy got on a plane that crashed, killing all on board. Would Barbara remain engaged in her work after losing someone who had become so close to her? Would she now choose to forgo the daily grind of practice that took her away from friends and play? Would the price Patsy paid in pursuit of her dream cause Barbara to refocus, concentrating on something other than the big picture?

Barbara never forgot the woman whom she considered a mentor, but she also didn't allow Patsy's death to stifle her own dreams. She continued to practice, continued to play dates in small venues and in front of small crowds. And, most important, thanks to her self-discipline, Barbara continued to push herself to get better each day.

More than her great voice and good looks, it was her expertise on a dozen different instruments that made her a star while she was still so young. Yet even as she began to build a legion of fans who came out to marvel at her playing everything from steel guitar to saxophone, she pushed to grow. She added new skills, such as dance and comedy. In a very real way, she was having the same kind of game-changing impact on the world of music and what was expected of entertainers in that field as Michael Jordan would soon have on the world of basketball. And both owed their success to their remarkable self-discipline.

Bowled over by her talents displayed during her live stage performances, NBC offered Barbara a chance to head-line her own TV series. Strangely, it almost didn't happen.

The grattitude of true self-discipline involves more than just sacrifice. It also embraces values. Those who are doing things the right way don't cut corners or short-change their principles. They cling to their core beliefs. Barbara had always performed gospel music in her live concerts so that others could see faith in action. When the network and pro-ducers balked at her ending her television shows with gospel music, Barbara didn't trade her values for money or addi-tional fame. She washed her hands of the deal and walked away. The powers that be called her back and allowed the religious music to be aired.

Like everything else she had done, Barbara's NBC series was a huge success — due mainly to her self-discipline. She constantly devoted extra hours each week to assure that every program in her series would reflect the same quality, energy, and values as her live performances. Her hard work was rewarded by great ratings and a loyal audience.

"The Sweetheart of Saturday Night" was on top of the world in 1984 when an auto accident nearly took her life. Her head and leg injuries were so severe that many feared she would not live through the first few days in the ICU. Certainly, most predicted she would never perform again. Yet the same drive that had made her a star drove her to overcome her injuries, and Barbara was back on the stage within a year, playing, singing, and—most remarkably—dancing. The steps on that journey were often painful, but the rewards made the pain worthwhile. And she did this by once again embracing the grattitude of self-discipline.

Though barely five feet tall, today the blue-eyed blonde stands as a musical giant who literally transformed an industry. At a time when almost every female act in the world was known as a "girl singer," she became the nation's most gifted live-stage entertainer. She sang, danced, and played a dozen different instruments. Her energy and charisma inspired a legion of young women, not just in music but in all fields. Her drive was embraced, and her vision of pushing the boundaries beyond one genre of music would pave the way for careers as varied as those of Alison Krauss, Shania Twain, and Reba McEntire. The winner of every major musical award from Grammy to Country Music Entertainer of the Year to People's Choice, almost a generation after her retirement from show business, she remains one of the most respected and revered names in the entertainment world. What made Barbara a star? In large part, it was a grattitude she embraced very early in her career—self-discipline.

Barbara demonstrates that hard work is a small price to pay for achieving an important goal. Yet for Barbara, it was never about selfish desires for fame and fortune. It was a calling. And even as she climbed to the top, Barbara bent down to lift others up. She helped other people with similar injuries recover and thrive, volunteering her time, energy, and talents. And maybe most important, by finding her own potential through her daily push to constantly improve her already incredible skills, she inspired a generation of others to follow in her example and brought great joy to millions who enjoyed her enthusiastic performances. Barbara's story tosses a bright spotlight on self-discipline and proves that this grattitude provides rewards that, when shared, make the world—and ourselves—better and brighter.

Giving Up Temptations

When I was growing up in the small, prairie community of Royal, Illinois, I had a friend, Rick Schmidt, who was tall and bright. Rick was the son of a farmer, and he was raised understanding the price and rewards of putting out effort. The Schmidt family always worked together as a team. Rick was driving a tractor and hauling hay when he was still in elementary school. He even got a city boy like me involved from time to time. Each summer, he and I were paid to cut weeds out of soybeans or bail hay. These tasks required such great effort in the hot sun that when the day was over, most of us couldn't wait to rest. I remember heading back to my house, eating supper, and spending the night lying on our couch, watching television.

Not Rick, though. As soon as the work was finished, he'd head out to the barn to give several more hours to something he dearly loved. Even on the darkest, coldest days of winter, Rick was in that barn, wearing layers of clothes, developing spin moves, fadeaway jump shots, and reverse layups. His dream was all about basketball. During these same days, most of the rest of us were inside our warm homes, spending hours involved with endeavors that had little to do with dreams or the big picture.

Without his glasses, Rick was literally blind. He also lacked speed and grace. Yet in spite of these shortcomings, or maybe because of them, he pushed each day to get better. He asked questions about the game. He sought out advice from those who understood each of the fundamental skills needed to master the game he loved. And then he worked and worked and worked. What was his driving force? What was the big picture he saw that the rest of us missed?

Rick wanted to play basketball at the highest level. That wasn't really unique. What midwestern farm kid doesn't share that dream? I spent hours thinking about making the winning basket in a big college game, but unlike others, Rick put feet to his dreams. Those feet would push him to achieving a complete focus on self-improvement. So while I shot a hundred shots a day working on my game, Rick *made* twice that many. He worked just as hard on ballhandling, moves around the basket, and positioning for rebounding. Rick fully grasped at an early age what few ever understand: luck doesn't really play into living dreams; rather, hard work paves the way to reaching them.

So when our high school careers were over and our tassels switched to the other side at graduation, most of us headed off to college knowing a great deal about sitcom plots. After all, we had spent many hours studying them while Rick was in the barn honing his basketball skills. Meanwhile Rick was rewarded with a full basketball scholarship to the University of Illinois, where he became a star. He would even be drafted into the American Basketball Association.

Yet Rick's success didn't stop on the court. His years spent in the barn working on his game paid off in an even bigger way. Because of his proven self-discipline, he was given a chance to work at a successful firm when his basketball career ended. His self-discipline there led to his becoming a wealthy man. And he took some of those earnings and endowed a scholarship at the University of Illinois in the name of the two hardworking, self-disciplined men who had inspired his efforts. One was his father, and the other was his first coach.

Barbara Mandrell and Rick Schmidt are role models for self-discipline. They didn't just dream dreams; they put into motion a plan to achieve those dreams. Like a runner training for a marathon, they gave up short-term enjoyment with the hope of achieving something they deemed very special. Living their dreams did more than set them apart from their peers; it also inspired countless others to follow in their paths, to give everything they had to live their dreams. And beyond just living their dreams and selfishly enjoying the fruits of their labors, Barbara and Rick then used their earnings and fame to reward others who embraced the same grattitude that had brought them incredible success.

A Musical Note

The church I attended as a teen in Muncie, Illinois, is the kind of church you would expect to be a product of the Farm Belt. The members are hardworking folks who pull their livelihoods from the land. Hence, as a group they understand self-discipline as well as any people I know. If they don't stay focused, they can't make a living.

When I was in high school, I had a church music director named Marion Minser. He worked hard to provide for his wife and two daughters, and he loved his job, but his real passion was music. Yet this slightly built, dark-haired man had never had a day of musical training. He couldn't read a single note from a songbook. He didn't even play a musical instrument. Thus, while a normal director would spend a few moments going over a new piece of music to learn it, Marion would devote days to this same task.

To get ready for each rehearsal, Marion, who sang by ear, had to first memorize all the parts of the choral specials—something that required hours of practice and took away a great deal of his personal time. Once he had memorized the soprano, alto, tenor, and bass lines, he had to teach all those parts to a volunteer choir that was often musically challenged. Week after week, Marion had to find a way to create a joyful noise from mouths that often could barely carry a tune. Year after year Marion persisted, and the music he created blessed thousands. All that time, he provided his services for free, giving his full effort in order to provide our church with a more beautiful worship experience. He never complained about the work. Never lamented giving up hours of his free time each week. And the smile on his face after each of our specials proved to me that Marion received a deep gratitude from his job. Yet his self-discipline used for his volunteer job was just the beginning of this man's devotion to what he felt was a calling.

During the week, Marion worked as a television repairman. He was always sensitive to any customer who couldn't afford to pay, and he reduced the cost of his labor. Thus, thanks in large part to the services he literally gave away and the time he spent working on his nonpaying job at church, Marion and his family lived in a very small home. As the state of their house deteriorated and the family grew, they faced a need for another bedroom and a more modern kitchen. Marion borrowed the funds to build the addition. Around the same time, our church was meeting in a school and working to raise the money to build a new facility. After much prayer, Marion gave the money for his home addition to the church building fund. Like the hours he gave to the choir, this was a sacrifice he wanted to make for the sake of something he believed was greater in value. Something he felt called to do. A dream that he saw was worth his sacrifice.

Unlike Barbara and Rick, whose passions were rewarded with monetary gains, Marion Minser never became a rich man. When he died, he still lived in the same small home he had chosen not to remodel. Yet decades later you can still see his influence in the small, white stone church he helped to build. His spirit is still there in the choir loft. People still talk about the way he lived his life and what a profound effect he had on the community. His self-discipline and drive to do things for others demonstrated what can be achieved when one lays aside personal desires for something greater. In our church, this grattitude created an atmosphere in which others began to give as Marion did, and everyone was better for it.

Self-Discipline Is Contagious

Those who worked with Barbara Mandrell worked harder because they knew how hard she was working. They gave more, spent more time in practice, and pushed for perfection because they saw Barbara modeling the same. They became better because of her self-discipline.

I played on basketball teams with Rick Schmidt. His teammates worked harder and practiced longer thanks to his influence. Rick's teams won in no small part because of his self-discipline and example.

People joined the choir and gave up a couple of hours each week thanks to seeing how much Marion gave to his calling. His pushing himself caused the members to push harder as well.

Yet why are those three examples so important to me? How have they impacted my life?

Though not writers, this self-disciplined trio — Barbara, Rick, and Marion — have heavily influenced my career in writing. Their fingerprints are on everything I have accomplished. They have helped me focus on the big picture and understand the rewards that come with sacrifice. The self-discipline I learned from them has become one of the most important elements in my work.

Inspired by these heroes, I can undertake even the largest writing project, dragging myself into my office even on days when I don't feel like working, breaking the project into manageable steps, working through all the editing processes, and pushing forward until the project is completed. I do so because I saw the results of effort like this in these three individuals. I am sure countless others have been equally inspired by them.

So you are embracing this grattitude for more than just yourself! Self-discipline is contagious, and once you catch it, you can't help but pass it on.

Hard Work

Now that we know what self-discipline is, we must ask ourselves how badly we really want it. Our self-disciplined heroes can inspire us to change and grow, but at the end of the day we each have to decide whether we will choose to make this grattitude part of our life.

There is an old proverb found in some African desert tribes that says, "Many have a thirst, but few want to pay the price to get to the water." In the case of the Maasai, that price is often having to walk forty miles to a watering hole, filling up a huge jug, and then carrying it back to the village.

Opportunity knocks, but success waits for a person to complete a task. It is a proven fact that those who only *dream* of success rarely *achieve* it. If we are self-disciplined, we will not only reach our potential; we will expand that potential.

But we won't get there all at once. Grattitudes are journeys. Barbara Mandrell might have had the drive to master a dozen different instruments, but she didn't do it overnight. It never works that way. Self-discipline is a series of steps, not one big leap.

At the beginning of the National Football League season, every team and player in the league wants to win the Super Bowl. Yet championships are won one game at a time.

Like Rick Schmidt, self-disciplined players and teams will focus on improving each day and mastering new skills consistently, keeping their eyes on the goal.

The grattitude of self-discipline is not a sprint; it is a marathon. Reaching the goal takes not only a vision for the big picture but also an appreciation for the small snapshots that will come together along the way to form that picture. In Barbara's case it was mastering new skills on an instrument, in Rick's case it was working on new moves in basketball, and in Marion's case it was learning new songs he could teach others. In my case it is developing a new idea and sharing it through a book.

What about you? What do you really want? What will you have to sacrifice to get it? I am sure Marion, Barbara, and Rick would tell you that giving up the things they gave up — the television shows, the hours on the couch doing nothing, the time talking on the telephone — was worth it. In my case, the years of barely making ends meet, of having to substitute teach and officiate basketball games, of not building our dream home or going on vacations, now seems like the best of times. Why? Because the dream has been realized, and therefore the journey to get there is something to celebrate.

But what if all the self-discipline leaves you short of your goal? What if you don't quite make it? Odds are that your growth experience as a person and the self-worth you have created through your efforts will give you a positive and happy outlook on life. You will recognize what you have gained in your journey and feel better for it. You will know your potential and never have to regret not giving the effort!

I know of very few old folks who say, "Gosh, I wish had been less self-disciplined." Most of the sages I have met say they wish they had developed that grattitude much earlier in life.

On the other hand, I can name countless folks who are bright, creative, and well-meaning. They have great plans and big dreams. The one thing they lack is self-discipline. As an example, I have seen several of my friends tackle the restoration of a car. They want to do a first-rate job, so they begin by taking the automobile completely apart. Then either boredom, frustration, or a desire to do something else sets in, and they go in a new direction. Years later they sell the car in pieces and talk about how they wished they had stuck with the job and finished the project. Finishing the job and reaching your goals while expanding your potential beyond expectations is the real reward of self-discipline.

Next Steps toward a Grattitude of Self-Discipline

I can see it in your eyes: you're ready to make the grattitude of self-discipline part of your life. We know it won't happen overnight, and we know it won't be easy—but that doesn't mean that we can't get started! There are some concrete steps you can take that will begin to grow your self-discipline.

Write down the name of the five most disciplined people you know.

List what they have accomplished by using their self-discipline, and list what they have had to sacrifice. Were those sacrifices worth it?

Now, using the positive influences you have just listed as your guides, set a goal for yourself. It doesn't have to be a big goal, but it does need to be life-changing in some way. It might be exercise, diet, Bible study, charity work, or prayer. It could involve productivity at work, a new job, more education, or being a better parent.

Once you have latched onto your new goal, list the temptations you will have to avoid to achieve it. By keeping those temptations in front of you and being honest about them, you'll make them less likely to sneak up and derail your progress. Everyone is tempted, but daily self-discipline can help us continue toward the goal.

Finally, list the steps or disciplines you will need to embrace to achieve your goal. For Rick Schmidt, it was sinking one hundred jump shots every day, while for Jesus' disciples it was likely telling the gospel to at least one new person a day. Your steps or plans will be a road map you can follow toward your goal.

A Final Thought

Rick Schmidt once told me that the key to his shooting was seeing the shot go in before he released it. I know that

Barbara Mandrell pictured her audience's reaction to her music even as she practiced all by herself. Marion heard the final choral performance before he taught his choir members a song and as he patiently memorized each part. As you work, picture the final result. Keep that image in your mind, and your efforts will not seem as taxing, and the trek will become much shorter. Change won't happen all at once or overnight, but with self-discipline you can become stronger each day.

GRATITUDE 2

GROWTH

No matter your age, it is never too late to begin a new journey. My father is learning Spanish as he enters his eighth decade of life. My wife went back to school and earned a master's degree at the age of fifty-two and a doctorate at fifty-six. Inspired by those who are continuing to climb new mountains, I try to learn something new each day. Human growth doesn't stop when our height peaks; it should only stop when we take our last breath. The bottom line is, we can't live by the statement "You can't teach an old dog new tricks."

There is one man who best represents the grattitude of growth, however: my good friend John Cathcart. John is one of the youngest souls I know. His energy and enthusiasm make him seem childlike, in the best sense of the word, to everyone he encounters.

I didn't meet John until he was almost seventy. By that time he had worked as a chemical engineer for nearly five decades. He was incredibly successful, a fact proven by his high-rise, corner office that looked out over the Dallas skyline. Born in Africa, raised by a Scottish missionary in Australia, but educated in the United States, John has a rather unique accent. His baritone voice is a fascinating combination of British and American, with a hint of Texas twang. His full head of snow white hair and his dapper goatee frame his blue eyes, and this, when combined with his aristocratic sense of style, makes him come across as the epitome of an English professor. He is a fascinating man, a world traveler, who has more stories of exotic and interesting places than anyone I have ever known. Yet John also possesses something else that lifts him above his peers: he accepted a new challenge that took him out of his fancy office and into the poorest regions on the globe.

In 1999 John, the man who had continually pushed himself to keep growing, was looking at retirement. He knew that after years of hard work he deserved a reward, but sitting back and reading magazines and watching television didn't appeal to him much. A woman from his church approached John one Sunday morning and asked if he would consider working for a few months as the interim director of a nonprofit organization that had orphanages in several developing nations. It seemed the president of WME (World Missionary Evangelism) had died, and the group was struggling to find its footing. John looked into the position enough to realize that many of the skills needed for this job were unfamiliar and that nothing on his engineering resume prepared him for this calling. But instead of passing on a new opportunity, he relished the challenges, studied even more intently than he had in college, and developed an enthusiasm for his new work. By skipping retirement and embracing a new cause, he also found the fountain of youth.

A decade later, now almost eighty, John is traveling the globe, visiting the poorest of the poor in jungles in India and slums in Africa, immersing himself in new cultures, delving deeply into biblical studies, and raising funds to push WME in new directions. Using all his life experiences, he has opened new missions in Kenya, Tanzania, Sri Lanka, the south of the Philippines, and even Burma. He has expanded the organization's established work in India, Bangladesh, and Nicaragua. Through his past contacts, he has also expanded WME's network of partners.

Watching John makes me realize how elderly men like Ben Franklin provided the energy to create an American Revolution. Their constant quest to grow and seek challenges gave them more than new mental growth; it also provided bursts of new vitality.

Many don't take on new challenges simply out of fear. John was a bit overwhelmed and scared when he accepted his new position. What if his leadership had taken WME in the wrong direction? What if a mistake he made had caused the organization to tank? Thousands of orphans would have been put out on the street. That is a heavy responsibility. Yet because John accepted the challenge, because he studied and grew, not only were the thousands of orphans provided with what they needed, but also the work grew to where it is now reaching thousands more.

The grattitude of growth requires us to swallow our pride and take risks. Growth means we might even fail. John knew this, and so did this country's founding fathers, but history's movers and shakers took a chance and changed the world. You can change your world too—but you can't get anywhere new if you're stuck in a rut!

John's example keeps me on my toes. John has taught me that the door of opportunity actually widens as we age! Because of him, I have tried new directions in Bible study, read more about international affairs, immersed myself in many cultures, and studied history more deeply. I have even started writing in a new genre—novels.

Each of us needs someone like John—a person who epitomizes growth and challenges us to reach new heights. Who is your John? Think of those around you who constantly embrace new challenges. Wouldn't you like to be one of them?

Search for New Vistas and Challenges

Consider Daniel Boone, a man of immense curiosity who never quit searching or growing.

Boone was a hero in the Revolutionary War who helped

explore the western frontier of his young nation. He traded furs for books that he read while on his explorations. He learned the languages of native tribes and founded and established communities in Tennessee and Kentucky. He led hunting expeditions from Florida to Missouri. He opened an inn, became a surveyor, and dabbled in what we would now call real estate. He was already sixty-five when the lure of adventure called him to leave Kentucky and settle in Missouri. A decade later, at the age of seventy-five, he organized a group of men to take a trip farther west. His goal, which he achieved, was to see Yellowstone. Along the way, he learned several new Native American languages and identified a score of unknown species of wildlife.

Even on his deathbed, Boone longed to see and experience just a few more things. He was a man who lived more adventures than almost anyone in American history, and yet his eyes remained focused not on what he *had* done but on what he *could* do.

What drove this American legend? Boone was a man who never wanted to quit searching or growing. Imagine: He was a king in his world. After founding Boonesborough— named, of course, after him—he could have kicked back and settled into the good life. Instead he was still pushing his horizons well into his eighth decade, meeting new people, facing new challenges, and literally blazing new trails. He died as he lived, looking forward with an unquenchable thirst to see and do more. His only regret was that he didn't have one more day to see one more new view or learn another thing about life.

Unlike John Cathcart or Daniel Boone, so often we become stuck in the past, remembering the "best" times. Perhaps it is a moment from years before—even in junior high or high school—when we won a contest or made a touchdown or dated a particular person. With great pride we claim that as our shining moment. There is nothing wrong with relishing moments in history, but if our growing stopped there, then those are really sad memories.

Yet it doesn't have to be that way. Legendary football coach Lou Holtz sums it up well. He was once asked to look back at his illustrious career and pick out his best moment. Holtz didn't have to think long. The little man with the overflowing trophy case grinned his toothy smile and replied, "Gosh, I hope I haven't had it yet."

God wants us to consider the infinite possibilities of our futures and never stop learning and growing as we move forward, which is a challenge. When I think of growing older and the great possibilities it holds, I am reminded of a woman who wrote lyrics to "The Battle Hymn of the Republic." As she aged, Julia Ward Howe became deeply involved in establishing rights for former slaves and true equality for women. In her eighties she still gave speeches, studied legislation, and read the latest books. When she was approached by others who looked at growing older as a curse and spent their hours wishing for their youth, she told them,

"The bowl of life grows sweeter as I drink it. All the sugar is at the bottom."

Now that Cathcart, Boone, and Howe have defeated that old statement "You can't teach an old dog ...," it is time to realize the other benefits of embracing the grattitude of growth. And this grattitude is not just for those who are older.

The Kim Zone

A wise, growing person never says things like "I will *never* do that" or "That would *never* happen to me." Such statements do not allow us to adapt as life changes—which it always does.

In 2005, Baylor University's women's basketball coach Kim Mulkey found herself in a position few would have guessed possible. The private school in Waco, Texas, which had no real basketball tradition, made it to the Elite Eight of the NCAA basketball tournament and was now just three wins away from a national championship.

Kim is a fiery, driven woman who stands about five foot three. When she is surrounded by her players, she is dwarfed. Thin, determined, her firm jaw usually set and her steely eyes focused, she is as tough as nails. At times she is so intimidating that folks fear approaching her. She is stubborn in her approach to the sport she coaches, she molds players to fit within her view of the game, and once she sets on a course she believes in, she rarely moves in a new direction.

With her incredible success record as a player and a coach, few question her philosophy either.

Kim hates to play zone defense. She has publicly stated on many occasions that zones are played only by the weak, and she had therefore stuck to a straight man-to-man defense each game. In her mind, a team is truly great only when they have mastered this concept. Yet as she looked at her next opponent in the NCAA tournament, she realized that her best opportunity for an upset would be to surprise everyone, step away from the mold she was known for, and employ the zone.

At first glance this change would seem as dramatic as Rush Limbaugh embracing Barak Obama, but when studied deeper, it becomes apparent that the coach never painted herself into a corner. While Kim had often blasted zone defenses in the past, she never made the statement "I will never play a zone." Thus the door was open for her to change and grow. Her refusal to let pride prevent her from doing the wise thing paved the way not only for the Bears' victory in that game but also for Baylor's first national basketball title a week later. Coach Kim was willing to grow and learn, and her growth led to wonderful new things for her team and school too.

As I've observed Kim Mulkey over the years, I admire and respect that while her principles don't vary, she grows within her profession. She has also helped me learn how important it is to adapt to situations in order to grow.

Stuck in One Place

A few months ago I was passed by a car that had a bumper sticker that said, "If it ain't the King James, it ain't the Bible." If that is the case, then I guess the Bible has only been around about five hundred years. That fact is that Christians often refuse to consider that God may be leading them somewhere new, and so they miss out on the opportunity to grow. Rather than read a translation of the Bible that might bring new insight, they continue to reread a passage in an older translation that makes little sense to them. Taken a step further, rather than reorganize a worship service to fit a new generation's spiritual needs, they keep doing the same things every week. It is in churches where I most commonly hear the statement "If it was good enough for my grandfather, then it is good enough for this generation too." That statement reflects the desire to stagnate rather than grow.

In Salem, Arkansas, the small church that my grandparents called a spiritual home had not grown for generations. The church was a victim of doing things the same way for way too long. In the early 1990s, the congregation brought in a young pastor with new ideas. Initially his "radical" concepts of community involvement and reaching out to a different class of people caused friction. Many established members even moved to other churches rather than share pews with those they considered beneath their social status.

Yet within two years—with a new order of worship, new programs, and a new outlook—the church established a vital ministry in the town. Its reputation became so strong that many people who had never been to church in their lives began to attend. Soon so many people were coming each Sunday that they were spilling out the doors for worship services.

Why did this happen? Because the congregation was not too stubborn to change—and as they changed, they grew!

Similarly, Jesus Christ shook up the world because he was willing to do things in a new way. He brought people to God by erasing needless rules and getting to the heart of the matter—something that upset the establishment. How dare he simplify the complex system they had established! How dare he make it easier to have a relationship with God! He scared the stubborn people of his era so much that they nailed him to a tree to silence his progressive thinking.

Today, what would many modern Christians do if Jesus came into their churches and tried to change their services and bylaws? How would they respond if he opened up their church to the modern-day versions of the woman at the well? Consider this: if everyone in church history had lived by the old thought "We are going to do it just like it has always been done," we likely wouldn't be singing "Amazing Grace" in churches today.

Change and Innovate

Sometimes the growth such innovation brings changes the world for generations afterward. In 1680, sixteen-year-old

Isaac Watts told his father that church was so boring, he wondered why anyone bothered coming. As the pastor of the little English church, Watts' father was probably deeply offended by the boy's remarks. Yet rather than give him a tongue-lashing, the man asked, "What do you find so loathsome?"

With the door open, Isaac boldly stepped in. He listed several things he would change, but the most important was the music. Singing from the book of Psalms and using the same six tunes every Sunday meant, said Isaac, that no one listened to the words. The message was being lost.

The elder Watts decided to issue a challenge. In modern language, he essentially told his son, "If you can write something better, then do it and I'll use it."

Isaac followed through, writing several tunes he thought might improve the worship. And his father, true to his word, allowed those songs into his church. Because of that experience, Watts would compose more than five thousand hymns. Songs such as "Joy to the World" and "When I Survey the Wondrous Cross" would start a musical revolution. For the first time, the Christian faith would have modern songs that reflected faith in a way people could relate to and understand. In a very real sense, Isaac was the father of gospel music.

A son's honesty, a father's challenge, and a push for change paved the way for others to follow. As a small church in England proved, tossing away our stubborn pride opens up unfathomable avenues of growth.

When we're in "the Kim Zone"—unafraid to try something new—we find that growth is a natural result. When we think like Daniel Boone, we keep looking for new things. When we keep pushing ourselves to grow, as John Cathcart did, we have the power to touch so many more lives. And when we accept challenges, the way Isaac Watts did, we can touch more lives than we can imagine. Don't confine your life to the words found on a bumper sticker or to a tradition that has lost its meaning; move forward.

Growing through Others

In November of 2003 I was sitting in the lobby of the Louise Mandrell Theater in Pigeon Forge, Tennessee, when I noticed the huge smile of an older African American man. He was happily standing in the corner, waiting for his wife to finish her shopping in the gift shop, when I introduced myself. After some small talk, I began to ask about his background. I discovered that he had been the first black student to enroll at Vanderbilt University, and his older sister had been the first student of color in an east Tennessee high school.

Since the show was about to begin, he had only enough time to tell me a small part of the story surrounding these historic moments in our country's existence, so I asked if I could take him and his wife out to eat afterward. He agreed, and our shared meal was a life-changing moment for me.

Our dinner conversation was pretty one-sided. I asked questions and let the man and his wife talk. I learned a great deal that night about intolerance and acceptance of race in our country. It was only as we parted company that he finally asked me a question.

"Why do you want to know this ancient history?"

I replied, "I'll never fully grasp what you went through when you were denied service and basic rights because of the color of your skin. I can't understand that because that kind of judging is something I have not gone through. But I can get a better idea by hearing the full story from your perspective."

He nodded, smiled, and shook my hand. Even as I watched him and his wife walk out the door, what he said remained with me, convicting me of my need to grow in the grattitude of acceptance.

Stubborn Pride Does Not Allow Detours — or Growth

But what happens when we don't follow those avenues for growth? Stubborn pride derails growth. It goes back to the statement about doing it the same way because Grandpa did it that way. This sets up roadblocks. It totally and completely stops the incredible grattitude we call growth. Consider this: Grandpa's way of doing things probably worked because he invented something new and exciting for his time. He'd probably expect you to do the same!

When I used to plan our vacation trips, I spent weeks making sure everything was in order. I doubt General

George Patton could have bested me when it came to laying out a strategic plan of operation. I had a time schedule, routes marked with highlighters, reservations, and the name of every good restaurant along the way.

Yet my planning pride was blocking my growth. I was always paying so much attention to my watch and making sure I met my goals that I was missing the wonders of the world around me. A traffic jam or a single wrong order at a cafe made me angry, as if my whole world were being turned upside down. I can't begin to imagine how much I missed because of this attitude.

A detour changed everything. One day I found myself slowly winding my way through a section of the Ozarks I had never seen. I saw a black bear rubbing his back on a tree trunk, a small herd of deer, and a flock of turkeys. On a road I hadn't intended to travel, I became so enamored with the landscape that I even stopped at a scenic overview, got out of the car, and spent sixty minutes taking in the panorama around me.

I discovered that in travel — and in life — it is not where you end up that brings growth but the journey.

Jesus spoke often about such journeys, and his lessons were for the young and old alike, for men as well as women. He taught that spiritual growth brings us new power — and he wants us to embrace that power today! Jesus made it clear that the Christian journey lasts a lifetime and that we will never stop growing if we continue to pursue him. In his last days on earth, Jesus told the disciples that after his death and resurrection, the Holy Spirit would teach them.

We are called to be alive and growing in Christ, and the living Holy Spirit loves and longs to grow and teach us.

Are you ready to let go of your pride? Are you ready to take a detour every day, exploring new roads and learning new things?

Are you ready to grow?

Next Steps toward a Grattitude of Growth

Admit your own mistakes. Like King David, who had to acknowledge his failures before he truly became a great leader, we cannot grow until we confess our own sins. It's never too late. That could mean something as simple as saying, "I'm sorry" to someone you have hurt or removing a personal roadblock like pride.

When you begin a new road, don't be afraid to ask for directions. It is hard to reach a new goal if you don't know where you are going. Ask for help, and you'll be surprised by how many folks will answer.

Give up the things that are holding you back. Don't hold on to to either traditions or possessions that have become meaningless or archaic. That is how churches and businesses die. It is also how relationships die. Remember that about half of the people in the colonies didn't want to break away from England in 1776. They were satisfied to live in a bad system and endure hardships rather than fight for freedom. What if the whole country had felt that way?

Quit habits that are hurting you. These bad habits can range from smoking to cussing to overeating. They can affect your spiritual and physical well-being. Do a short inventory and see if anything in your world is holding you back.

Don't be afraid of detours. Sometimes the view from a new, unexpected road is exactly the view you need to see. Make a list of places you might like to go or skills you might like to learn. Even if they seem off the beaten track, they might be exactly where you need to go.

Make a list of things you want to do before you die. You are never too young or too old to have goals. There is always something out there worth seeing, doing, or learning. These goals will push you to grow.

List how you plan to achieve your goals. With this road map, you will have a path to growth.

Identify those who can help you with your dream. List who they are and what they can teach you, and ask them if they are willing to help you on your journey.

Latch onto people who you know are growing and doing it as naturally as they breathe. Study them and ask their secrets and find out their motivations. They can be your teachers, and what you learn from them can allow you to teach others.

A Final Thought

Never say, "I am finished learning" or "I know all I need to know." Each day calls for a forward-looking attitude. Remember, your tombstone might be life's diploma—after all, it marks departure from this world—but the report card of your life is the extent to which you fulfilled your potential.

Courage

I met Larissa Vigil when she was in college. She was short, tanned, brunette, with piercing blue eyes and an athletic build. The first time we talked, I found out she was considering a career in either coaching or sports medicine. That all changed when she took a church-sponsored mission trip. In Kenya she discovered the plight of older orphans in the third world. When she came back to the United States, Larissa told others about the young women who were being pushed out onto the streets and forced into prostitution or crime because they had nowhere else to go and no one who cared enough to take them in. Their "long-term" future usually meant dying of AIDS before the age of twenty-five.

Rather than wait for someone else to do something, Larissa sold everything she had and moved to Kenya. She set up a program to educate teenagers, giving them job skills and finding college scholarships for them. She stood up to those who tried to exploit these children, refusing to back down even when threatened with physical violence. Imagine this five-foot-four kid making this move. Imagine her white face in a crowd of Africans. Imagine how much she stood out. Who in their right mind would do something like this? Who would take this kind of risk?

By the time she went to Kenya, I had gotten to know Larissa well. I knew that her courage was fueled by a passion to right a wrong. This had to be the same kind of courage that caused American Revolutionary War hero Patrick Henry to bravely sacrifice his life for a cause he believed in. This had to be the kind of courage that fueled the zeal of the groundbreaking missionary Lottie Moon and the explorer Christopher Columbus. Each of these people was willing to stand out and possibly fail in order to do something others would not do.

Larissa was excited when she got off the plane in Kenya to begin her new life. If I had been in her shoes, I might have turned back in fear, but she didn't hesitate. She was there to save lives, and she didn't want to waste a single minute. Not long after she arrived, she toured the great slum of Kibera. With people literally living on top of one another, with raw sewage flowing down the streets, with drug addicts and thieves surrounding her, she turned to a member of the police force and asked the man if he had ever been into the heart of the depressed area. When he told her no, she answered, "Shame on you. There are people there who need you too." In a few minutes, both of them left the slum's one semi-safe street and headed toward its center. Larissa's courage to make that trip once opened the door for the policeman to begin a daily trek into that area to make sure children were not being abused and people felt some kind of safety.

Another time Larissa stepped between an orphan and an abusive adult who outweighed her by at least a hundred pounds. Like a mother lion protecting her cubs, she wouldn't back down until she was sure the child was safe and well away from the adult. In fact, she took the child with her to her own small home.

Larissa told me she went to Africa because she believed she is needed there. If you believe something strongly enough, she said, then you need not fear. The key to having courage might well be in believing in something with all your heart. Those with true courage are those who feel they have been called to do what they are doing. If you are living a calling, then you likely have courage to do things you otherwise would not even consider doing.

Larissa has become one of my role models for the grattitude of courage. She refuses to shy away from a challenge, no matter how daunting or dangerous. If Larissa can walk into the most dangerous slums, I can speak openly about my faith and my beliefs. And because I have told her what she means to my life, I must strive not to dishonor this incredible young woman. In my calling, I must just as strongly write the truth and push to venture into subjects and territory that might seem unsafe.

Courage Catches On Like Wildfire

There are countless historical accounts of men who have stood up in battles only to have entire squads follow in their footsteps. The same was true in the civil rights movement. For years no one stepped forward, but when Rosa Parks refused to give up her seat on the bus, others came to stand (or in this case, sit) with her.

If Hollywood had written the story of Rosa Parks, it would have been tossed out by the movie studio. The powers in the motion picture industry would have never accepted a tiny, frail woman as the symbol of courage. They would have instead rewritten the script and placed a hulking man in the lead. This person would have possessed the power of a superhero. He would have stood in the face of authority, and his mere size and strength would have caused the status quo to shake in its boots. Yet when the defining moment in the civil rights movement occurred, it was a diminutive woman who challenged long-standing tradition. It wasn't rippling muscles or invincibility that fueled her courage; it was simply the knowledge that she was right and society was wrong. Within a generation of Rosa refusing to give up her seat, true civil rights legislation was enacted, schools were integrated, and America grew to become a place where dreams could be dreamed by children of all races.

Would Rosa have possessed such great courage if the prize she was seeking had been something she didn't believe in? Probably not. As with Larissa, it was her belief or calling that gave her courage. Thus the key to possessing the trait the Cowardly Lion so badly wanted in *The Wizard of Oz* is finding your mission.

Yet there is another great lesson to be learned when looking at the lives of two women as different as Larissa and Rosa. When Larissa went into the slums to see what she could do in the places no outsider ventured into, a policeman followed. When Rosa took her seat on the bus, thousands got involved in working for civil rights. It is quickly apparent that when one stands up with courage, a team follows that person's example. But it takes the one making the first step.

Moving Forward with Everyday Courage

In the case of Larissa Vigil or Rosa Parks, courage meant confronting people and circumstances that were potentially volatile. Yet courage is also exhibited in much smaller, everyday ways. It takes courage for a baby to take its first steps. It takes courage to begin a lifestyle change such as giving up alcohol or going on a diet. It takes courage to make a move to change jobs. It even takes courage to fall in love.

Anywhere there is risk, there is a need for courage. This grattitude is a must if you are going to completely embrace the first two grattitudes presented in this book—self-discipline and growth.

At first glance, Keisha Pittman would have appeared to be just another student. She was bright, outgoing, and popular, but there was nothing that really set her apart from dozens of other young women who possessed those traits. What would ultimately shine the spotlight on Keisha was hearing news that her life might not have been just beginning; it might well have been ending.

Keisha was a senior in college when she noted a lump on her neck. She didn't want to be sick. Many looking at the lump might have tried to ignore it. They might have adopted the old "if I close my eyes, it will go away" philosophy. That is what fear can do. It can cause people to ignore realities. Yet for Keisha, denial wasn't an option; Keisha decided she would face the problem head-on. So knowing that the lump could bring news she didn't want to hear, Keisha had the courage to seek the truth. She went immediately to the doctor.

The school physician immediately ordered a CAT scan. Less than a week later a vibrant young woman was given the news that she had lymphoma. Suddenly finals or having a date to the big game seemed to be the least of her worries. She was staring at death.

What would your reaction be?

For many, the initial reaction is to give up on normal living. They take on the bunker mentality. They dig a hole, isolate themselves, and try to focus on not dying. Keisha displayed her courage by doing just the opposite. She saw her fight as a calling, and that calling gave her the courage to fight cancer in the open. She displayed in the bright sunlight what the disease was doing to her. She tossed a spotlight on it. Why? She felt a need to inspire anyone else who might have been going through what she was going through.

I have known many people who battled cancer, but few have displayed the character and courage of Keisha. Through regular online blogs, complete with haunting photos, she shared every honest step she took. She wrote of her fears, her heartaches, and her small triumphs. She held back nothing.

Keisha's writing showed her courage in unique ways. She stayed in school and stayed focused on her homework and her student job. When her hair fell out because of chemotherapy, she courageously shared with her friends that change in her life. And, like so many with cancer, she found joy in the little things she had missed in life.

Keisha demonstrates that folks who display real courage don't gripe. They don't complain. They don't ask, "Why me?" They just march forward, striving to reach a goal and ready to meet any roadblock without flinching. They echo the words of Dorothy Thompson, the American journalist who once stared down Adolph Hitler: "Only when we are no longer afraid do we begin to live." Keisha discovered the fullness of life when facing her death. If she had not had the courage to continue living and sharing that life with others, that wonderful realization likely would have been lost on her — and on the countless thousands she inspired.

Keisha's courage was easily seen, but there was another, often-overlooked group that showed great courage as well. When people are in trouble, many of those around them become frozen in panic or fear. Often only one person races into a lake to rescue a victim while scores watch from the shore. When someone has a serious illness, many friends hide rather than help. Why? Because they fear they won't know what to say or do, or they fear that what they see will hurt too much to bear.

In Keisha's case, people from all over campus stuck by her. They knew that the price of doing this might be pain and anguish. They knew they might invest a great deal into something they might lose. But they did it anyway. In taking this subtle step of courage, Keisha's friends learned more about life and the joys of embracing each moment than they learned from any college course.

Keisha beat her cancer and, thanks to her courage in facing the disease head-on, she inspired thousands. An old saying goes, "Courage is not knowing what is around the corner but going there anyway." While Larrisa, Rosa, and Keisha had no idea what was around the corner, they chose to go nevertheless.

When we live the grattitude of courage, we can't help discovering what really matters in life. We discover it around a corner where others fear to tread.

Courageous People Admit Their Mistakes

My grandfather often said, "When you find yourself in a hole, quit digging." While it takes courage to face monsters such as illness, poverty, or prejudice, sometimes it takes even more to face our own mistakes. Few link courage and the admission of guilt or fault. But the Bible is filled with stories about just such a thing. The courage of the confession is a theme that plays out in the stories of Moses, David, and countless other biblical heroes. They had to fess up, and that took some humbling. Admitting mistakes takes courage, and not admitting them shows signs of cowardice. And this form of cancer poisons lives each day in ways that few can imagine.

When we admit that we have failed or messed up, the issue usually goes away much more quickly than it does if we try to find a way to rationalize or hide the error. For some reason, however, it is a part of human nature to try to bury the mistake rather than acknowledge it.

Adam and Eve's son Cain couldn't understand this. Abel and Cain both brought gifts to God. Abel's gift was accepted, but Cain's was not. In fact, God challenged Cain to do better. Cain took out his anger on his brother, killing him and hiding the body. When God asked what had become of his brother, Cain launched into a bit of double-talk, digging himself even deeper into his hole.

This was not the first time humans had tried to shift blame to avoid punishment. As the Bible reminds us, Cain's folks also tried to point the blame in other directions, when they were caught eating a certain fruit. So it seems that using the "I was wrong, but it wasn't my fault" excuse has been a part of the human condition since the very beginning.

I do pretty well avoiding certain kinds of foods I don't need—until I see an advertisement on TV. As I watch a commercial pitchman telling me just how great Blue Bell ice cream is, I start to feel myself weakening. A few minutes later, when my wife comes in and sees me holding a big bowl of Cookies 'n Cream, I try to explain that it's the *television's* fault. The excuse doesn't work any better for me than it did for Eve. Using it is a small admission that I lack courage.

Not everyone makes excuses, however. In 1952, when Dwight David Eisenhower ran for president of the United States, one of the chants heard from his supporters was, "Ike is right." Yet eight years before, on June 5, 1944, as hundreds of thousands of Allied soldiers, sailors, airmen, and marines readied to launch what we know as D-Day, Eisenhower wondered if he was right. Would the invasion of France work? Would the Allied forces be able to push the Nazis back from the beaches of Normandy? Those questions haunted him as he prepared to send thousands to their deaths.

If the actions of June 6 had failed, General Eisenhower wanted to make sure that no one blamed the men who were putting their lives on the line in this operation. He also didn't want any of those who had drawn up the various facets of this plan to suffer criticism. On June 5, Ike put pen to paper and prepared an apology in case of failure. In that note that never had to be issued, Eisenhower took full responsibility for the battle's loss.

Yet he took things a step further. When the beaches were taken — when the general could have taken credit for the war's most decisive victory — he deflected the congratulations to those who had landed on those beaches and parachuted behind the lines. Ike was prepared to take the high road no matter the outcome.

True courage is ready to face any external challenges — and any internal failures too.

Simple Courage Brings Respect — and So Much More

As was pointed out in the examples of Larissa and Rosa, people who display courage are reacting to a calling. So be sure of this: you aren't called to be courageous for no reason. Courage brings benefits that the cowardly will never understand — and can never earn. How quickly we admit we messed up — how quickly we put this grattitude into play — says a great deal about how much we want someone's respect and how much we deserve it.

When my younger son, Rance, was in junior high, he had a friend over to visit while I was working on a tight deadline for a book. It was crunch time for me, so I asked the boys to play in the far side of the house and keep it quiet. Several times they drifted out of the room and made enough racket that I had to stop working and remind them of what I had asked. Finally, they actually broke an antique glass in the kitchen. By this time I was boiling with rage.

I raced into the kitchen and noted what they had done. I glared at Rance and demanded an explanation. I thought his reply showed a lack of respect, and I reacted by slapping him. My action, which was so out of character, shocked him. I sensed he was ready to apologize for his actions.

Yet before he could tell me *he* was wrong, *I* fell to my knees and begged his forgiveness. I was wrong to ever strike him, and I wanted him to know that. I have never felt as bad in my life as I did at that moment. Even though Rance offered me an escape by telling me his actions were wrong, I wouldn't accept it. I was the one who overreacted. I was the one who did the most harm.

Ultimately, my humbling of myself at that moment showed Rance just how much I loved him. We still have a bond that is built on trust and respect — a bond that was strengthened when I immediately admitted I was very wrong.

Thank God I had the courage to admit my mistake. If I hadn't, then my calling as a parent would have suffered. Thus in everything you do, in every position you hold, you are called to have the courage to be honest. In today's world, that kind of courage seems to be in short supply. But remember the examples of Larissa and Rosa; if we display courage, even the kind that humbles us, others will follow in our footsteps. This is a grattitude that really is contagious.

The Courage Found in a Fresh Start

Admitting mistakes leads to a clean slate and a new beginning. A fresh start makes a world of difference. It means that you have not only assured others that you know you messed up but also admitted it to yourself.

Having the courage to admit our mistakes also gives each of us the chance to use our mistakes to help others. If we hide our mistakes, we can't be a role model who keeps others from falling into the same traps that snared us. Often, people who have navigated tough times become the best leaders, and they have invaluable lessons to teach others.

If you don't speak French, you probably will never be able to teach it. Similarly, if you pretend you have never made a mistake, you can't help someone who is struggling with a mistake themselves. When we have the courageous grattitude to admit our mistakes, we often become effective leaders—in a way that a cowardly person never could.

Courage Is …

What is courage? It is all about not just doing what frightens us but also doing what is very hard. The thing that is most difficult for most people at home, in their social lives, and at work is admitting their mistakes. If you can do that, then you probably have the courage to climb the highest mountain, speak in front of thousands, and ride the double-loop roller coaster at Six Flags.

Mark Twain once said, "It is curious that physical courage should be so common in the world and moral courage so rare." Hence, the sign of the greatest courage is not fighting for your own life but fighting for someone else's. Each of us sees wrongs in the world around us, but how we react to those wrongs defines our courage. Will we attempt to make them right?

Next Steps toward a Grattitude of Courage

If you have something that keeps you awake at night, write it down. If you are scared of an illness, then go to the doctor and find out if there is anything to fear. Whatever it is, after you write it down, list the ways you can overcome or confront this fear — and then find the courage to take those steps.

Share your fears with others who are going through the same thing. Tell them how you confronted your fears and how finding courage proved a blessing. Your honesty will help others find the courage to change, and even to become leaders themselves.

Take a stand for something you believe in. List the things that matter most to you and that you want to see change — things like local homelessness or the lack of clean water in Kenya or a cause you learn about at church. If you see a wrong, have the courage to set it right; without courage, evil will continue to flourish in our world.

List the mistakes you have made that you have either

ignored or tried to blame on others. Be honest and judge yourself as others would. Above all, don't rationalize your actions. Don't wait for your deathbed to confess — try to make things right here and now. When possible, seek out the person you have hurt and apologize. If you can't speak to them in person, write a note or make a call.

A Final Thought

Franklin Roosevelt is credited with saying, "The only thing we have to fear is fear itself." Several years ago I received a letter from the Internal Revenue Service. It came on Friday, and my fear of being audited prevented me from opening it until Monday. When I finally worked up the courage to tear open the envelope, I discovered a check. I had overpaid them. Don't let fear cheat you out of the gifts of life. Whether the thing that scares you is big or small, find the courage to confront it and move forward. When you embrace the gratitude of courage, any journey you begin alone will soon gather a host of others for the trip. This is a gratitude that will make you a leader who shapes and reshapes the lives of others.

GRATTITUDE

4

HUMOR

Humor is one of the most important and most overlooked of all human qualities. Laughter and joy help us make it through tough times. Life is far too short to wallow in misery—and company doesn't love misery. People are drawn to happy folks and shy away from those who are grumpy. Happiness is also a great stress reliever. And from a practical standpoint, even though scientists have yet to pinpoint exactly why, happy people have fewer illnesses than those who are unhappy.

Remember Janie from the introduction? Janie was in her thirties when diabetes struck her blind. After her husband divorced her, she functioned independently for several years before meeting a happy, outgoing man whom she would marry. Since Steve could see, he became her eyes.

One night at a church banquet, a woman sitting across the table from Janie and Steve struck up a conversation.

"As I understand it," she said to Janie, "you were blind

when you met Steve—so you've never seen your husband, right?"

As soon as she uttered those words, the woman gasped. What had she said? How would Janie take it? The woman really felt as though she had put her foot in her mouth.

Though Janie couldn't see the worried expression on the woman's face, she sensed it. With her eyes twinkling, Janie paused for a moment, then, in a tone that suggested concern, answered the query this way: "Why, is there something I should *know*?"

The room grew very silent until Janie, after waiting the appropriate amount of time, burst out laughing. Soon everyone followed her lead. She had diffused an awkward moment and infused it with laughter and joy. More than making herself comfortable, Janie's joke made everyone else in the room comfortable—and better people too! Yet that is just the beginning of what this grattitude can do in your life.

Dying Laughing? Not a Bad Way to Go!

On March 3, 1993, Jimmy Valvano—best known for coaching North Carolina State's men's basketball team to the national championship in 1983—was dying. In less than a year, cancer had consumed the forty-six-year-old's body. On that night at Madison Square Garden, Valvano received the ESPY Award for courage. He was so weak, he had to be helped to the podium, but once there he somehow found the strength to give a speech that has become one of the most popular YouTube videos ever. His words moved millions to tears. By the time he finished his remarks, he had not only received a long, tearful ovation but also started a movement that has raised tens of millions of dollars for cancer research.

Years later Valvano's own daughter was saved by that very research.

On that night, when he was staring death in the face, Jimmy V, as the world knew him, began his speech with several side-splitting stories that had the audience literally crying with laughter. He took listeners through a parade of events in his life that, from his perspective, were great learning moments because they were so funny. He spoke of his first coaching job, when he gave a super speech to fire up his team. The problem was, he used one of Vince Lombardi's speeches, and he was coaching a group of Scarlet Knights. Thus, when he told them to win one for "their God, their family, and their Green Bay Packers," the kids were a bit confused. Then, when he raced to the door to knock it open and lead them into their first college basketball game, he found himself flat on his back because he didn't realize the door opened in and not out. For ten minutes he told stories like that, and those in the audience soon forgot that they were looking at a man who was dying of cancer. What they saw was a person who loved life and loved to make people laugh.

Then, just when everyone in the crowd was ready for his next funny anecdote, Jimmy V made a very serious point about cancer research and the importance of treasuring each day of life. Long after the night was over and Valvano died, the jokes he made still bring smiles and laughter, but the serious lesson he delivered in the midst of his humor is what made such impact and still resonates today. I feel sure that if he had started with the lesson, he wouldn't have made nearly as strong a point.

That night at the ESPY Awards, Valvano used humor to show a crowd who almost didn't want to look at a sick, dying man that he was still a strong, valiant fighter. Humor didn't just draw people in; it changed their perspective — and then it motivated them to action. Thanks to that speech, more than fifty million dollars has been raised for cancer research through the V Foundation. Countless people are living, thanks to a man who could still use humor when facing death.

Humor truly can change the world.

That Guy's a Nutt!

Grady Nutt was a Baptist preacher whom I met when I was a college student. He often came back to Baylor University's homecoming and with his jokes would entertain those of us working registration lines. Yet he taught important life lessons with his laughs. His sermons made me smile even as they caused me to think about the Bible in a fresh way.

Grady was the man who first made me realize that Jesus smiled a great deal. The joy with which Grady lived his life showed me the importance of keeping a smile on my face and in my heart.

Grady was a tall, thin man with big eyes and a larger smile. I always thought he looked a little bit like another very funny but spiritual man—Tennessee Ernie Ford. Grady's voice was larger than life, and when he spoke, he did so not just with his mouth but also with his whole body. His hands moved to emphasize each word, his face contorted to become the characters in his stories, and he rarely stood still. His way of speaking was so personal, he could be talking to two thousand people, and I still felt like I was the only one in the room.

I remember the time he gave a message on the famous Bible story about the woman at the well. In that story, he became Jesus. Rather than just say the words "Those without sin are free to toss the first stone," Grady picked up a large stone as he talked. He tossed it up and down in his right hand as he paced and set up the story. Then, when he was ready to present the lesson of not judging others, he tossed that rock against a wall as hard as he could. That was when he said, in his east Texas twang, "Now, those of you who have never sinned can pick up that rock and go to work."

Another time, he was speaking of how he believed that God must have a wonderful sense of humor. He then contorted his rather unusual features into a silly face and added, "If he didn't, why would he have made me?" In a very real way he made us laugh, but, because he showed us the warm, friendly side of his nature, when he wanted to, with a story like the woman at the well, he could easily make his serious point. Why? Because thanks to his humor, those who knew him were ready to listen to him. In fact, as with other great warm, wise folks, such as Will Rogers, folks were drawn to him.

Grady once made me laugh when we were talking about having to fly from city to city. Suddenly his face grew worried, and he leaned close and said, "You know, God doesn't protect you in airplanes. The Bible says just that, so it must be true."

I was confused. I wondered if this was another one of his serious lessons, so I whispered, "Really?"

He grinned and answered, "Yep. Jesus said, 'Low I am with you always.' He didn't say anything about high!"

As I watched this man charm audiences with great humor and then interject a powerful, life-changing, soul-transforming point in the midst of the laughter, I decided that I wanted to adopt this man as my role model. He got it! He understood the power of an easy smile and warm story.

Grady died before I had a chance to tell him how much he had impacted me, but to this day I try to share with others what he taught me. A good joke is the fastest way to open a door to the soul, and a hearty laugh brightens so many lives. Whenever I get too serious, whenever I am convinced that life is nothing but pain and misery, I think back to a joke, a play on words, or a story that Grady told. The memory of Grady's smiling face lights my way whenever life seems dark.

When we open our eyes to the world, we can find reasons for joy. A squirrel can make us smile, but we have to take the time to watch its antics. We can read timeless humor, such as the short story about Adam and Eve written by Mark Twain, but we have to open the book. A joke can make us grin, but we have to listen. Yet if we just watch, read, and listen, we will find that laughter is indeed the best medicine—and it's a cure we can give to others as well as ourselves.

Finding Balance

William Arthur Ward once said, "A well-developed sense of humor is the pole that adds balance to your steps as you walk the tightrope of life." Navigating life when things are going well requires a certain degree of balance. But when times are tough, laughter becomes even more important.

Beth Nance was a student at Baylor University in the 1980s. The young woman was bright, beautiful, and charismatic. Her eyes sparkled; she had a Miss America smile and a dancer's grace when she moved. Yet in one day it all changed. A throbbing pain in her leg turned out to be Ewing's sarcoma, a form of bone cancer that, at that time, killed ninety percent of those who contracted it.

As a pump shot high doses of chemotherapy drugs into her system, Beth bravely continued her classes, participated in her sorority, and spoke to church groups. She even won the title of the school's homecoming queen.

One rainy fall day, she put on a parka, grabbed her backpack, and as she used her crutches to pull her weary body across campus, the full extent of what cancer was doing to her smacked her right in the face. Soaking wet, she slowly worked her way up three flights of stairs to the floor where her English class met. Since she was early, she sat down on a bench outside the classroom, finding herself alone in the large landing except for one young man who was also waiting for a class to be dismissed so he could go into that room.

Tired of dealing with the parka, Beth yanked it over her head. When she did, her wig came with it. The action revealed the extent to which chemotherapy had changed the student's appearance. As the boy across from her gasped, Beth reached down, picked up the wig, and then with a huge smile said, "See what being an English major will do to you!"

Beth constantly used humor to push through tough times of fighting cancer. When her dermatologist called and wondered why she hadn't made an appointment or ordered a new prescription, she explained, "I'm on chemo. This stuff is amazing. You wouldn't believe how clear my skin is — this is what you should have been prescribing all the time!"

At the very time when cancer could have moved people away, Beth pulled her friends in and made them feel comfortable through her humor. But she used it to open a door to teach great lessons. She made high school kids laugh about her fight but then added, "Cancer might kill me, but I will not die doing something stupid like getting drunk and crashing a car or overdosing on drugs. Life is too precious to be stupid in the way you use it." After they had laughed with her, the kids were ready to consider the sobering lessons she taught. She understood what Jimmy V knew: a smile can take you through the toughest of times, and humor can open the door for you to change the way others look at the precious nature of life.

Humor Opens Doors and Increases Influence

For many years I led singing in a small rural church. A nurse sat in the second row of the right-hand pews, and whenever I looked in her direction, I was greeted by a huge smile. Her smile caused me to smile. When Julie wasn't there, the church wasn't quite as bright or cheery. Her single smile helped to light the entire building!

According to the old saying, you can catch more flies with honey than with vinegar. We know this is true in our everyday lives. If you walk into a store and have a question, do you approach the person who has a serious look and a stiff demeanor, or do you choose the person with twinkling eyes and an easy smile?

It's about more than just ourselves, of course. When we choose the grattitude of humor, it helps other people see us, and the world, in a new and better way.

Sitcom Wisdom

The grattitude of humor can also provide a safe way for people to engage the serious matter of life. My youngest son once told me that when he grew up, he wanted to provide for his children the same kind of home I had given to him and his brother. I should have simply accepted his compliment, embracing the words and basking in their glow, but I had to know what he *really* meant.

The explanation that followed my query surprised me.

"Dad, living with you is like living in a television sitcom. At times you bumble around, you make strange faces when we say certain things, and you really draw out life's awkward moments. In other words, you make us laugh!"

In my son's eyes, I was like the fathers on *Leave It to Beaver*, *Happy Days*, and *The Cosby Show*. Was this a compliment? Then, as I pondered his words, it dawned on me that the fathers on those shows might have been the butt of jokes and mishaps from time to time, but they were also the ones who, after the laughter died down, were listened to for serious advice.

I decided I liked being the funny guy who occasionally was looked to for wisdom. It was far better than being ignored.

Next Steps toward a Grattitude of Humor

The grattitude of humor is like a fireplace on a cold night: people are drawn to bask in it. Humor is like a door that opens to reveal trusted wisdom. Does humor improve your life, or are you always on the outside looking in? When folks think of you, do they grin or remember something funny you said or did? Do people look forward to the next time they'll see you so they can smile some more?

If not, maybe it's time to go to a mirror and start practicing your smile.

Try listing situations or relationships in which you come off as too serious or just downright unhappy. What triggers those negative vibes? What can you do to put a smile on your face and joy in your heart? Do you need to get rid of some negative media forces in your life or even find a new job?

Think of those you know whose smiles are sincere, and then list why you think they are happy. Do they do anything that you could incorporate into your own life?

Try to begin each day with a thought that makes you smile, and end each night by writing down a reminder for your next morning's smile.

A Final Thought

Not long after the Lewinski scandal, President Bill Clinton was asked to attend a conference of evangelical pastors and field their questions. The president must have felt as though he had walked into a lion's den. One of the first questions asked that day was, "How can you still attend church?"

The president paused, dipped his head, and then in a very serious tone said something like, "Have you ever known anyone who needed to be in church more than me?"

The answer was humbling, but it also brought a few quiet laughs as the pastors considered his words. It was a serious joke that defused an explosive situation and revealed a truth. It didn't change the wrong that the president had done, but it did open the door for dialogue and perhaps some forgiveness.

As Janie, Jimmy, Grady, and Beth prove, humor has the kind of power to open doors. If you want to be welcomed into a lot more places, use a warm smile as the key to those doors.

GRATTITUDE

5

TENACITY

My cousin Barbara possessed blue eyes that flashed with the energy of a cloud-to-ground lightning strike. She was thin, but strong and tough as nails. She also possessed a sharp wit and a strong will. I loved being around her, because I sensed that if things got tough, she would be the one in our clan to lead us to higher ground. I was sure that of all the Collins clan, she was the one who could be stopped by nothing. But I was stunned into silence when Barbara was struck with multiple sclerosis (M.S.). After all, she was a twenty-eight-year-old mother of three. Just three months before, her husband had died of cancer. It simply wasn't fair.

When faced with the news, Barbara could have given up. She was holding a baby in her arms when she was told her M.S. was the aggressive type. She was alone with obligations that would have brought many healthy people to their knees. Yet she simply set her jaw and asked, "What do I need to do to prepare myself for this war?" And fight she did. Even when the disease confined her to a wheelchair, she kept fighting, and she continued to embrace her role as a mother. She would not be stopped from living by the insidious nature of the disease. For almost thirty years I watched her try every treatment available. Chemotherapy made her sick; physical therapy drained her strength; prescription medicines led to painful bloating. Yet through it all she kept fighting. Even in the days before this cruel illness took her life, she was still trying to find a way to get out of bed. She was determined to walk again and inspire others with the same disease. In other words, she never lost the tenacity that drew me to her when we were kids.

Also, late in her life, when she was confined to a nursing home, Barbara never stopped working hard and trying to serve others just like she had served her children on days when the disease should have kept her flat on her back. Though moving her wheelchair was difficult for her and navigating the hallways left her completely drained, she volunteered to deliver the daily mail to the bedridden patients in the home. If they couldn't read the letters, she read to them.

Tenacity isn't about mere survival — it's about survival for a greater purpose. True tenacity is fueled by a calling.

Barbara's never-give-up attitude has been a profound inspiration to me. Sometimes when I'm discouraged, I think of Barbara, and my whole attitude changes. I told Barbara several times she was a hero to me. I strive to honor her by continuing to take advantage of my physical blessings, refusing to complain about my small aches and pains and using my mobility to do something constructive.

Barbara never managed to walk again, but she was a winner because she didn't give up. She embodied tenacity. Tenacious people always push forward and never see any obstacle as permanent. When the scoreboard shows they are way behind, they play just as hard, clinging to the concept found in 2 Corinthians 4:8: "We are hard pressed ... but not crushed."

Following a Calling

William Carey is known today as the man who created the modern missionary movement. With a vision to reach people in India, the cobbler and teacher gave lectures on the need to evangelize the world. Most of the people who heard those lectures told him to go back to his shop and school and forget his dream. A noted minister, John Ryland, even grew so upset with Carey's passionate speeches that he said, "Young man, sit down; when God pleases to convert the heathen, he will do it without your aid and mine."

Yet the tenacious Carey refused to quit. In 1793, at the age of thirty-two, he left England with very little money and support to follow what he believed was his calling.

Carey spent four years in India before a single person even listened to his message. For the next two decades, only a few more came to accept the faith Carey was offering.

During that time, his wife died, he lost all support from England, and he was forced to work as a teacher and printer to feed his family.

Every time he was knocked down, he got back up and, like a champion boxer, answered each new bell. Nothing could get him offtrack. He was there to share the story of Jesus, and he continued to do so in the face of rejection few have ever known. When he died at seventy-two, the total of souls converted to the Christian faith through his work was but a handful.

Since that time, however, the movement he began has seen hundreds of millions of lives transformed. If Carey had not embraced the grattitude of tenacity, the missionary movement that has changed the face of Christianity in India and around the world would likely not exist.

Never Give Up

We don't have to fight a disease or be called to preach in a foreign country to be tenacious. Tenacity is a grattitude each of us can embody in whatever situation of life we find ourselves.

In the late 1980s, I developed a vision for a book I wanted to write that told the stories behind the songs of Christmas. Since Christmas music was such a vital part of the holidays, I figured everyone would be interested in knowing what inspired the carols of the season. I quickly found out I was wrong. My book proposal was rejected by more than two dozen publishers — both big and small —

over the next decade. Everyone told me that it was simply an idea that wouldn't work. Yet for reasons few understood, I kept sending the book proposal out.

Finally, because of some other successful writing projects, I was able to convince a publisher to take a chance with my idea. In 2001, after more rejections than I care to remember, *Stories behind the Best-Loved Songs of Christmas* was released. It is still selling and has even spawned a number of sequels. Ironically, that much-rejected book earned me the title "bestselling author."

I have had a lot of folks ask me why I stuck it out so long when the logical choice would have been to give up writing. The answer involves faith coupled to calling—in my mind, that defines tenacity. If you have faith in what you are doing, you can be tenacious in your pursuit of your dreams. In that sense, my cousin, who displayed tenacity to such a great degree, deserves a lot of the credit for this book becoming a bestseller.

Let me assure you, when you achieve the dream, the long trek and great sacrifices almost seem like a walk in the park. You wouldn't trade them for anything.

Barbara might have never walked again, but the pursuit of the goal enriched the last thirty years of her life. Perhaps some of the experimental treatments she tried might even one day save others. Hence, the quality of life she embraced during her fight was much higher than if she had just given up and gone to bed.

Carey might have saved only a handful of souls, but in his mind, those souls were worth his effort. Thus tenacity is about more than just reaching a goal; it is a life-changing lifestyle.

Pride Is Not Tenacity

First Corinthians 13 is all about grattitudes. The eleventh verse speaks about the danger of pride: "When I was a child, I spoke and thought and reasoned as a child does. But when I grew up, I put away childish things" (NLT).

Some folks get tenacity and stubbornness confused. They lump them both together. In truth, they are at opposite ends of the spectrum. Tenacity pushes people forward, while stubbornness holds them back.

Stubborn pride is a childish thing. Babies cry when they don't get their way. Sadly, many of us never outgrow this behavior. We allow pride to stifle our tenacity. We would rather stubbornly wait for something to happen than going and making it happen.

A friend once told me, "If I'm going to get a new job, someone will call me." He prayed each night for a job, but he didn't write up a resume or check the want ads. He felt that the job he needed would come to him even if he just sat at his home and did nothing.

I had another friend who wanted to get married, yet she refused to join a singles class at Sunday school, allow friends to set her up with dates, or even go to mixers. She told my wife many times, "If I'm going to get married, someone will find me." But it was difficult for anyone to meet her when she always stayed at home!

Tenacious people don't hide from the world; they enter it and act. Prideful people *want* to leave their mark on the world, but it is tenacious people who actually do.

The Dream

Martin Luther King Jr. was born in 1929 in completely segregated Atlanta, Georgia. Before he learned to speak, he was exposed to the fact that there were two different cultures in America. One, the world that held the most promise, was reserved for those whose skin was light. Those with darker skin were relegated to a lower place in society.

What made this man different from millions of others born into the same kind of bleak world? What caused him to believe he could knock down the wall that had been in place for decades? It was tenacity.

King participated in marches in which he was beaten. Those who beat him were trying to get him to submit to the old segregated ways. He was jailed countless times in an attempt to not just silence him but also get him to give up. He was cursed and called names in order to humiliate him. Yet he kept going. Nothing would silence him.

My cousin did not quit trying new treatments because she believed she would one day walk. William Carey didn't allow his lack of success to keep him from believing that the message in his heart needed to be shared. King was equally convinced that if he did not give up, his dream would be realized.

No man's dream is any better remembered than that of Martin Luther King Jr. Yet King didn't just write speeches about dreams; he marched for it. He gave his entire adult life to what he saw as his calling. While he lived for that dream, he also died pursuing it. Yet that dream changed the country and set in motion the concept that another tenacious man started a hundred years earlier. King understood the grattitude of tenacity.

Mark Twain once said, "Twenty years from now you will be more disappointed by the things that you didn't do than by the ones you did. So throw off the bowlines. Sail away from the safe harbor. Catch the trade winds in your sails. Explore. Dream. Discover."

What is your safe harbor? And what is waiting for you on the other side of the water? Do you want to reach the dream? Then you have to get the boat moving. Believe me, I know for a fact that the journey is also worth it.

Next Steps toward a Grattitude of Tenacity

Take a piece of paper and write down your dreams. Don't worry if they seem crazy.

Pick a dream and write down the steps for making that dream happen. If you want to go back to college, decide how you will do it. If you want to get a promotion at work, chart your course. It is much easier to stick with something if you have a goal clearly in your mind. Your steps may change as you move forward, or they may be a bit vague at times, but to reach a dream, you must have a plan.

Keep track of rejections and the roadblocks that you meet in your quest. They can become motivators. If you believe deeply enough in what you want, you will continue to push past them, and looking back on the ones you have already defeated can motivate for the long haul.

Keep a list of people who inspire you through their tenacious efforts to live their dreams. In my case, the first one who came to mind was Barbara. Yet there are scores of others too. Who around you has never given up? Who has pushed for their dreams even when the odds were completely against them?

Find a role model who tenaciously pushed toward success. Learn everything you can about that person, and put his or her proven pattern to work in your own quest.

A Final Thought

Each of these cases cited in this chapter, and scores that you know in your life, reflect the old children's story of the little train that was trying to climb the big mountain. The train kept saying, "I think I can, I think I can." Those are the most important words a tenacious person can say.

GRATTITUDE

6

FORGIVENESS

John Lewis was born the son of sharecroppers on February 21, 1940, outside of Troy, Alabama. He grew up on his family's farm and attended segregated public schools in Pike County, Alabama. When he was a child, his world was strictly divided by the color of skin. There were places he could and could not go simply because of his race. Thus he knew that the opportunities afforded him in America would be limited not by intelligence or talent but because he was black.

If anyone had a right to refuse to forgive, it was John Lewis. Yet, inspired by the civil rights leaders of the 1950s, Lewis decided to help correct a wrong and try to open the door to allowing people of all races to participate in the American experience.

Beginning as a student at Fisk University, John Lewis organized sit-in demonstrations at segregated lunch counters in Nashville, Tennessee. In 1961 he volunteered to participate in the Freedom Rides, which challenged segregation at interstate bus terminals across the South. Following in the footsteps of Rosa Parks, Lewis risked his life countless times by simply sitting in seats reserved for white patrons. Many times he was severely beaten by angry mobs. Little did he know that his actions were about to bring him face-to-face with a man who saw Lewis as little more than an animal to be smashed.

Like many of his generation, Elwin Wilson saw men such as John Lewis as the embodiment of unwanted and unwarranted change. Wilson felt that his skin color made him superior to every black person in the world. So he was naturally determined to stop any act that might lead to the integration of society. Fueled by anger that had morphed into rage, Wilson stood up with a mob trying to block the integration of a dime store lunch counter. While many in that group hurled profanity-laced insults, Wilson took it a step further. He attacked twenty-one-year-old John Lewis.

Lewis refused to fight back. Following the principles he had been taught in Sunday school, he turned the other cheek. Knocked to the ground, his face bloodied, and now fearing for his life, the college student prayed that his attacker would walk away. While Wilson stopped the beating, he was not finished with his acts of intimidation. Grabbing an egg, he cracked it over the black man's head. The next day, the world was vividly introduced to his actions, as scores of newspapers presented a black-and-white photograph snapped during his attack. To some, Wilson instantly became a local hero for giving Lewis "what he deserved."

The battered Lewis walked away, but he didn't give up. For years he continued his struggle, even as his rights continued to be denied. At the same time, others like Wilson attacked Lewis. They hounded and beat the young black student. They cursed and berated him. At every turn, in places like Selma and Atlanta, they blocked his way. What if Lewis had responded in like manner? What if he had embraced a vendetta? What would he have gained, and what would America have lost?

Instead Lewis stayed the course and peacefully worked toward his goals. Lewis adopted the philosophy that those who were attempting to harm him simply were not fully aware of what they were doing. He didn't blame them. Rather he pointed out that these men and women were a product of their times and environment. When others demanded he adopt the axiom of meeting physical violence with physical violence, he opened his Bible and pointed to Matthew 5:38–42: "You have heard that it was said, 'Eye for eye, and tooth for tooth.' But I tell you, Do not resist an evil person. If someone strikes you on the right cheek, turn to him the other also. And if someone wants to sue you and take your tunic, let him have your cloak as well. If someone forces you to go one mile, go with him two miles. Give to the one who asks you, and do not turn away from the one who wants to borrow from you."

From Anger to Grace

By 2009 a seventy-two-year-old Elwin Wilson had grown much wiser than many of his peers. He now was ashamed of his past and wished he had never been a part of the KKK. He was especially haunted by what he had down to Lewis. Driven by guilt, Wilson traveled to Washington, D.C., to apologize. Standing in front of a man he had once beaten and humiliated, he admitted how wrong he had been. Lewis opened his arms and welcomed Wilson as if they were old friends. A bridge was built as these two very different people met, far into their journeys, on level ground.

From the 1950s until today, Lewis has always turned the other cheek. He never plotted to get revenge; instead he has looked for ways to move forward. Even when those who cursed and beat him tried to derail his every move, he forgave them. Now even a man who once hated him has become his friend. Such is the power of the grattitude of forgiveness.

Pulling the Wedge Out

On June 15, 2005, Jared Cheek was killed in a car accident. The other driver, Rob Stalling, was drunk and lived. At the trial, Jared's mother asked the judge to keep Stalling's sentence to the minimum. She argued that he could do more good telling his story than spending his days in a prison. Thus the judge assigned the young man to probation.

"I will miss Matty [what she called her son] every day of my life, but blaming Rob and not forgiving him will not bring him back," Pam Molnar told the *Leaven*, a Kansas City, Missouri, newspaper.

Earlier this year, Molnar accompanied Stalling on visits to high schools in the Kansas City area. After she introduced him, he told students about the fatal car crash and the harsh realities of drinking and driving. Together the mother and the driver have vowed to prevent others from suffering the way they have. Pam Molnar's faith prompted her to offer forgiveness rather than retribution, and now she will never be a victim of the cycle of revenge.

Put yourself in Pam Molnar's shoes. What would be your reaction? How would you respond? How difficult would it be for you to forgive?

Martin Luther King Jr. said, "Forgiveness is not just an occasional act: it is a permanent attitude." Life is far too short to waste your time plotting a dark vendetta and missing out on the joy and love that come from walking in peace and wholeness. It doesn't make any difference if those you forgive don't respond to your act of charity—what matters is that you are getting rid of that cancer in your life and moving forward.

If someone has hurt you, remember the words of Christ on the cross: "Father, forgive them, for they know not what they do" (Luke 23:34 AB). Remember the story of John Lewis. Embrace forgiveness as a gratitude, and you will free yourself from bitterness and the need for revenge. When you toss away old vendettas, watch as acceptance, forgiveness, and grace begin to fill your life!

Don't Forget Job's Response

In the Old Testament, Job loses everything yet amazingly does not curse God. In fact, he continues to thank God for what little he has left. I have friends whose daughter suffered a Job-like experience. At a party she was unknowingly drugged. After she left, the drug took effect, and she was involved in a car wreck. Though she was not badly injured, the man driving the other car was killed. Tossed in jail, charged with vehicular homicide, and unable to afford a seasoned lawyer, this young woman found herself looking at thirty years in prison.

For the next five years, Emily lived in a tough prison reserved for the worst offenders. Rather than grow bitter, she opted to embrace the old proverb of blooming where she was planted. Behind those walls, she prayed for freedom and set to work tutoring other inmates as they sought to earn their high school and college degrees. Her unselfish work behind bars impressed the warden. In time, because of her continued efforts to improve the lives of others, her story was covered by the national media. This led to a new look at her case. This time the courts set her free. Justice was finally served.

The real lesson is not in her fight for freedom but in her forgiveness of the system that wrongly imprisoned her. She is not bitter and now looks at her time behind bars, as painful and unfair as the experience was, as being filled with blessings. It was there she was able to help others. It was there she was able to fully display her faith. It was there she found out how strong she really was. The day she refused to let her circumstances kill her was the day she truly began to live.

Get Over It

When forgiveness is delayed and wounds are allowed to fester, the consequences can be disastrous.

The lack of forgiveness poisons our relationships. Slight wounds and insults become insurmountable hurts. The longer we refuse the grattitude of forgiveness, the harder it becomes to embrace it. Often the solution is painfully simple — as my son's friends say, "Just get over it!"

In my life, I have been wronged a few times. I have been accused of things I didn't do. My first reaction was anger. The next was, naturally, to wish that those who had wronged me would suffer even more than me.

A few years ago I witnessed something that deeply disturbed me. Members of a group I respected were out in public acting in a manner that presented them in a very bad light. Their behavior was beyond rude and had become disgusting. Several around me pointed it out and wondered why no one was coming down on these young people. When I got home that night, I fired off a note to the head of this group, who was not in attendance on that evening, and in that note I told her what I saw and how much it bothered me.

I stated in my note that it was private and not to be

shared. I was writing and sharing this information because the group's actions might hurt its image in the community. I felt sure that if this leader knew of this behavior, she would want to do something about it.

I immediately received a call informing me that my views were not needed or wanted. She further stated that her group could do whatever it pleased. I was surprised by the reaction, but it did not hurt me. Yet when my private note was read to the group and one member was told, "You can choose being friends with him or this group," I was deeply hurt. I felt betrayed, and my anger almost boiled over. I felt I had reason as well.

To this group, my image was badly damaged. The leader had put me in a place where they would never like or trust me. Should I hang on to the bitterness? Should I allow it to rule my life, and not see the other things the group and their leader had accomplished? No. I may not agree with what she did, I may not understand her actions, but she was dealing with the situation from a different perspective than I was. I cannot judge her by my standards. In fact, according to what I have read in the Bible, I can't judge her at all. Thus the only action left for me is to forgive her and move on.

Over the past several years I have therefore written several notes of praise to her regarding various things she has accomplished. I have singled her out when she has achieved great things. I have even used those examples in my writings and speeches. And never once have I asked her for an apology. Forgiveness is not about getting even; it is all about letting go and moving on.

The Christian Life Refuses Revenge

Once we get over something, we still need to forgive. Christians are called to emulate Jesus, and Jesus was all about forgiveness. Think about what he said on the cross. Did he call out to his followers to revenge his death? Did he beg God to hurl a few lightning bolts?

No! Jesus said, "Father, forgive them, for they know not what they do."

Without Jesus, hate carries on from generation to generation. Jesus taught through both parables and his life that it was time to fully embrace forgiveness and see it as a positive force. In Jesus' world, absolutely everyone — Jews, Gentiles, rich, poor, men, women — was included in the offer of forgiveness. Jesus tried to alter all the narrow-minded thinking that was so common with those who wore their religion on their sleeve. He tried to get folks to see the big picture, and that meant forgetting old vendettas.

Next Steps toward a Grattitude of Forgiveness

Make a list of those who have hurt you. Be specific about what you think they have done to you, the pain they have caused you, and how it has changed your life.

Write down the significance of the harm you have suffered. Decide if the action or your reaction caused the greatest pain. Usually it is the latter.

Look again at your list and begin to forgive those who have hurt you. Don't ask for them to pay a price for that forgiveness—just do it. That means not worrying about whether they admit their mistake or own up to their faults. Christ forgave his tormentors from the cross. It is doubtful you will have to endure that much pain in your act of forgiveness.

Once you have taken the steps to forgive, write down how those acts changed your life. Have you gained new friends? If so, list them. Have you enhanced relationships with those you love? What blessings are yours that you did not have when you were harboring thoughts of revenge or retribution?

A Final Thought

The dictionary tells us that compassion is a human emotion prompted by the pain of others. More vigorous than empathy, compassion gives rise to an active desire to alleviate another's suffering.

How different would the world be if Christ had asked for revenge rather than forgiveness from the cross? Christianity would not be the faith that reached out to others in love; it would be the religion that sought out and provided justice with a hateful sword. In the long run, we are measured not by our wealth or position but by our compassion. The latter only really begins to bloom when we freely offer forgiveness.

GrATTITUDE

7

TEAMWORK

Each of us is part of a team. Whether we like to admit it or not, we rely on others and others rely on us. What matters most is not how we stand out as individuals but rather how we make the team better with our time, energy, and gifts. When we make the team better, that same team gives back to us in our moments of need.

The lesson that each individual is called to be more than an individual is exemplified by Shalee Lehning, a point guard who played basketball for four years at Kansas State University and now plays in the WNBA. Shalee is not a large woman. At a bit over five foot seven, she is strong but lean. She is quick but not fast. She is not so much a pure athlete as she is an example of a person who worked hard to enhance her modest God-given skills. If you were to line up ten women from the pro league and ask someone to pick out the one who they thought was not really a pro player, she would likely be the first one chosen.

So why is this brown-eyed former high school homecoming queen constantly surrounded by young girls seeking her autograph? Why was Shalee so successful at making others look better that her college number was retired?

If you look through the Kansas State record books, you will not find her leading the list of the school's scorers. Also, she was never a great three-point shooter. Where her name pops up first is as the school's assist leader. What does that mean? Essentially, Shalee was the person who passed the ball to someone who made the points. And she did it more than anyone else in school history. She also led all rookies in the WNBA in that often-overlooked category in her first year in the pro ranks. In other words, Shalee became a star by literally passing the spotlight to others.

At the ceremony where Shalee become the first player at Kansas State who was not a scoring leader to have her number retired, thousands cheered as her number 5 jersey was lifted into the rafters of the gym. Over the deafening roar, a newspaper reporter asked the basketball player what it meant to have her number honored in such a way.

"I've always thought there were five on the court. There isn't just one," she replied. "There are five of us out there at a given time, which is why I picked number 5. For that number, I hope people know that this honor does not exemplify Shalee Lehning. That's for the team, the program, the university, anyone who helped get me to where I am today. I didn't do any of this on my own. It's always been a team."

Shalee's attitude provided Kansas State with more than just wins. It gave the school an unselfish sports icon. Because she was seen on a national stage as someone who put others first and herself second, many parents steered their high school kids to attend the school she attended. Although Shalee didn't know it, her values made her a recruiter for the school. Yet that was just the beginning. Thousands, including many reporters, tried to find out why, in the era of "me first" athletes, Shalee put such an emphasis on team. The answer proved to be a recruiting tool for another group.

Shalee explained that it was her Christian faith that caused her to look out for others. It was her faith that forced to her to think about giving before receiving. It was that faith that made her want to lift her teammates and diminish herself. And it was her faith that caused a number of folks to look at their own lives and then join the team she viewed as the most important in her life.

We're all on a team — and those of us who embrace the grattitude of teamwork become leaders who make others, and ourselves, better. True team players also become the greatest and most followed leaders.

Teams Create Friendships

Remember the old childhood lesson "There is no *I* in team"? Team is about working together. If you bring others in on each new effort you attempt, you will find that you will grow stronger with them. If you join a team, then the sum total of the efforts that you and your teammates make will have a much better chance of succeeding. If you go it alone, you will likely lack vision. When you are part of a team, you see the whole picture.

In Shalee's case, her team won a league championship. She couldn't have done that on her own, and Kansas State couldn't have done it without her passing.

Bestselling author Margaret Carty revealed another important factor in playing for and with a team. She said, "The nice thing about teamwork is that you always have others on your side."

There is something uplifting about having others around in both the good and the bad times. We need to be able to share our victories and defeats with our friends. If you are not a part of the team, this can't happen. So being part of a team means you will never be alone.

Teamwork also keeps you grounded. It means you will be less likely to compromise your morals or principles. When you know that others are looking to you as a role model, you will live up to a higher standard. If you surround yourself with friends who are of high caliber and put those players on your team, then you will have a much better chance to embrace those same values.

Being part of a team makes you more like Christ and more likely to do the kind of work he did, including reaching out to those in the greatest need. Why does it do that? Because you look out for others before you look out for yourself. You seek a shared glory, not an individual one. You care deeply about not just the strongest around you but also "the least of these." That is the kind of person people are drawn to.

The Power of Team

Team is often defined as a number of persons associated in some type of joint or community action. It is a group of people who are united by a cause. At its simplest, team is played out in games. Yet in its deepest form, team is all about relationship.

I had a huge crush on Nancy Sorrell in college. She was a cute, outgoing dynamo, independent and self-confident. What really drew me to her was the way she befriended those around her. She always had time to talk or give a hug. Those gifts are grattitudes that everyone loves.

Cancer claimed Nancy more than twenty years ago. Yet in her brief thirty-three years on earth, she taught me a lifetime of wisdom about the incredible value of friendship. She showed me that nothing—not poverty, time, schedules, or even disease—can separate true friends. Nancy understood that friendship and team are linked. She knew that from experience. She realized, as she watched a team of doctors and nurses fight for her life and saw her family circle up to support her, that team was essential.

Nancy's life was all about team. Her first team was her family. Because Nancy constantly sought out ways to serve them, her brothers and parents were always there for her. They supported her in the tough times because she had been there for them through each success and failure. She would take off at a moment's notice to help her mother or father if one of them became sick. She would drive for hours to share a special moment with her brothers or their families.

The next team was her friends. Even when she was battling cancer, she would find the energy to go to weddings, showers, and other special occasions. She remembered birthdays and anniversaries.

She was dying and knew it when she still found enough strength to drive several hundred miles to celebrate a friend's daughter being crowned a college homecoming queen. I was there that night watching a weak, drawn, and pale Nancy smile, give out dozens of hugs, and constantly put the spotlight on a young woman named Beth. She could have begged off. But she didn't because she realized the importance of friendship and team. You see, Beth had cancer too, and Nancy wanted to make sure Beth saw that cancer could not and would not hold Nancy back. Nancy felt that if she had not come, then Beth's spirit might have been dealt a blow that would have hindered the younger woman's cancer fight. In "Shalee" terms, Nancy was there to give Beth an assist. What was most amazing about Nancy that night was, she took the time to make a dozen new friends. And with that smile, she brought them onto her team. Each would soon learn something from her about the precious nature of life and the joy of being surrounded by friends.

Nancy had another team in the end. It was her doctors and nurses. She gave herself to them. She allowed them to do whatever they needed to do to help her fight cancer. She never complained, and she encouraged them when they had to give her bad news. She refused to allow them to feel down just because they were fighting a fight they knew they couldn't win. In fact, when the doctors and nurses grew sad as they spoke of the terminal nature of Nancy's disease, she often prodded them into telling her about a patient they had who had beaten cancer. And she congratulated them on saving that life. She saw that as her role on the team. She was the encourager even when her team members could offer no encouragement to her.

In her final months, Nancy used cancer as a bridge to help her befriend new people and share her strength with others who had been touched by the disease. Like few I have ever known, Nancy truly understood that being a friend meant you were part of a very special team.

Because of her loyalty, most of Nancy's friends never deserted her when she was battling cancer. To this day, because of Nancy's defining the nature of friendship and team, I make daily efforts to ensure that the people I love know — through calls, emails, and thank-you notes — how much they have impacted my life and how glad I am to have them on my team. Nancy's influence remains so strong that

I call or email a friend whenever their image pops into my head. Her example also gives me the courage to even go to people who are hurting so badly that I have no words to ease their pain. And isn't that when a team needs to embrace a teammate the most?

Before Nancy died, I was able to tell her that I was a better person and a better friend because of her. I actually said, "Thanks for allowing me to be on your team." She laughed and told me that I could have probably picked a better one. I assured her that I was honored to be on hers.

Nancy defined friendship when it is coupled to being part of a team. It means that a person needs to be forgiving, honest, direct, and gracious. When I asked her if she ever felt it was unfair that she was struck with cancer three times, she replied, "I would rather have this happen to me than to someone I love." That defines the true nature of a team member as well as any statement I have ever heard, and it showed me why she was such an important part of so many different teams at church, in her hometown, and in her family. We all want folks with faith as our friends and as a part of our team.

No One Is an Island

If *Animal Planet* were to do a special series about my life, the narrator would describe me as a pack animal. Think about *your* pack—your immediate family, your friends, your coworkers, and so on. Each of us relies on many others, from the teller at the bank to the clerk at the grocery store to the folks who pick up our garbage.

Most of us are not loners or hermits. We are joiners. We like to be part of a group or a team. But those who actually *believe* they need no one else are mistaken in that belief. They too can lose a loved one or be hit by a major disease. No amount of wealth or power can change the fact that we rely on others constantly and that we're part of a social web.

We need friends. We need mentors. We need guides. We need folks we can call and talk to. We need those who will be honest with us and encourage us. Such people are our friends, and friendship means we are embracing our place on a team.

Nevertheless, some of us persist in believing the lie that we are totally independent. We don't need anyone, and no one needs us. Whether we admit it or not, this is usually an easy way of getting ourselves off the hook when it comes to helping others, since we don't "owe" anybody anything.

But life usually teaches us that such a view is a lie — and sometimes the lesson is painful. Like most of us, Hall of Fame quarterback Joe Namath had to be taught the nature of both football and life. Humility did not come naturally. A brash and confident teen, he once thought he had all the answers. During his freshman year at the University of Alabama, this belief was pounded out of him.

During a fall practice, Namath was running the scout team for legendary coach Paul "Bear" Bryant. Bryant called a specific play, but Namath felt he knew something better. In the huddle, he drew up his own play and ran for a touchdown. As he was returning from the end zone, Namath casually tossed the ball to the coach and said, "How'd you like that, Bear?"

Bryant expected Namath to work as a member of the team. The coach had called the play to prepare his defense for what the team would be seeing during their next game. Yet Namath had decided to run his play and had wasted precious practice time. His behavior showed that the young man had no respect for his coach nor a healthy understanding of team. Bryant was steamed.

Storming over to Namath, Bryant instructed the young man to run a quarterback draw and that under no circumstances was he to change the play. Then, without telling Namath, the coach informed the defense what the play would be. A second after the snap, Namath was buried by linebacker Leroy Jordan. As the quarterback hit the ground, he fumbled the ball. Bryant walked over, picked up the pigskin, and strolled over to the woozy Namath. As the now-humbled quarterback struggled to rise, the coach tossed him the ball and asked, "How'd you like that, Joe?"

Joe Namath never forgot that lesson. For Joe to succeed, he had to play for and with his teammates. He eventually won the Super Bowl with the New York Jets. He became known as the quarterback who bought meals for his linemen and as the guy who thanked his teammates for every block they made. Namath understood what it meant to be part of a team, but it was a lesson that didn't come easy.

At last Namath had reached the point where he could say, "Football is an honest game. It's true to life. It's a game about sharing. Football is a team game. So is life."

I know that Namath's example holds true in my career. I couldn't have written this book alone. Those who provided this book with their stories of inspiration are the most valuable players on this team. Then there are my editors, my publishing company, the marketing and publicity team, the sales staff, those who work at bookstores, and even those who buy and read this book. They are all part of my *Grattitude*-team, and that makes this book, like every book I write, a "we" project!

The "I'm in Charge" Attitude

There is an old saying that it is lonely at the top, but that is usually only true because those at the top stop letting others into their world. Not only is this exclusionary attitude short-changing those who close the doors and build the walls, but it can also have a dramatic effect on the professional success of businesspeople who fall into this practice.

In the middle of the Roaring Twenties, Henry Ford was king of the automotive world. For almost twenty years he had targeted the needs of the motoring public. By keeping things simple and affordable, he had put much of America on the road. The Model T, also known as the Tin Lizzie, was inexpensive, easy to maintain, and reliable. With a brilliant but simple philosophy, Ford cornered eighty-five percent of the nation's new car sales.

The Model T was the first automobile most Americans owned. Yet as new jobs and higher salaries fueled the expanding industrial revolution, drivers began to want a comfortable and refined vehicle. The men surrounding Ford attempted to tell the industrial icon that the Model T was outdated and ill suited for the next generation of buyers. Yet, as ruler of his world, Ford refused to listen, and competitors' cars began to outsell his.

By 1931 the Ford Motor Company was no longer dominant. Did Henry learn his lesson? Did he listen to the concepts of others? Not really. He continued to stubbornly insist on doing things his way. By the time he died, his once-powerful company was in third place and falling fast. The only thing that saved the company was a grandson who brought in a team of brilliant young minds, including Robert McNamara and Lee Iacocca, who understood the new market because they were a part of it. Working together, these men from vastly different backgrounds discovered what needed to be done and set to work rebuilding Ford with a new line of cars and new, less individualistic ideas. Management became inclusive rather than exclusive.

Consider the life of Ford. When he began, he was in touch with the common man. He understood him. He was also the first major car builder to integrate his plants. Yet when the money rolled in, he fell out of contact with those he once accepted on an equal basis. It almost cost him his company. Each of us runs that danger. If we exclude people or groups, we lose a part of our ability to understand the world around us. Team is an inclusive concept, not an exclusive state of mind.

Christ's Team

When Jesus began his ministry, he formed a team. The twelve he chose each had special talents, distinct experiences, and unique motivations. When mixed together, their differences became their strengths. Jesus taught his disciples about individual responsibility and team play.

When we stick the name of Jesus on marquees in neon lights, we forget that he was a real person with real friends. The real Jesus shook hands, hugged those he loved, and taught mighty lessons in everyday ways. He got rocks in his sandals just like everyone else. In the way he humbly went about the work of his Father, he presented to us the importance of relationships with family, friends, and coworkers. Jesus was perfect—and he was *still* part of a team!

Jesus showed us through example how to nurture relationships if we want to have any hope of changing the world. He took the time to listen to the woman at the well and offer her a spot on God's team if she was willing to give up her old lifestyle. He recruited new team members wherever he went. Could he have changed the world on his own? Sure—he had the power of the ages at his beck and call! But Jesus came to teach the world how to live in relationship and work as a team, a lesson that quickly spread far and wide.

A Man Named Paul

Saul of Tarsus was incredibly arrogant. Before he was struck blind on the road to Damascus, he was sure he needed no one. His goal was to wipe out the team that Christ had put together—and he was going to do it all by himself. Yet when he became Paul the apostle, he immediately wanted to become part of a team.

You don't have to look far to understand what team meant to Paul. He wrote letters explaining it. In those letters, he thanked his team for their support and hard work and provided them with game plans for how to better play the game of life. His writings to the churches might have singled out some for special thanks, but they also included this vital message: "You are one body." What is a group of people who are one body? A team, of course.

You can tell, in Paul's writings, that he took the time to get to know his team members. He understood when they needed to be praised and when they needed to be taught a lesson. He began the book of 1 Corinthians by thanking and praising the members of the team. He then asked them to stop arguing because it was hurting the team. Over and over in his letters to the churches, Paul used the word *we*. Today, more than nineteen hundred years after his death,

Paul's life, actions, and words are still bringing new members to his team.

Consider something else about Paul. To many, he would have been thought of as an outsider. He was a citizen of Rome. He had worked for the government. He had once sought to punish Christians for their faith. Thus he would hardly have seemed suited to become part of a team that followed Jesus' teachings.

So those who came to know and accept Paul as not just a member of this team but also a team leader had to forgive him of his past transgressions. They had to open their hearts and trust him when he had once given them no reason for that trust.

Teams are not made up of people who are perfect or folks who are just like you. In fact, a team is best when the members have different talents and different perspectives. The key is for all the members of the team to be seeking the same goal.

There is no parable better known or more repeated than that of the good Samaritan. An injured man of a different race and faith is ignored by travelers until finally one person is moved to pick him up, tend to his wounds, and pay for his care. When you embrace acceptance as a grattitude, you will be the one who stops to aid the person whom everyone else ignores. This action will become as natural as breathing.

In business, this means opening up the team to new

employees. In families, it means accepting new members who might come from a different place or even race.

Unlock Doors

When Paul was Saul, he had the "god of your world" complex. That complex has destroyed more successful people than any other single attitude. Scores of entertainers, politicians, businesspeople, and even preachers have taken a quick plunge simply because they thought they knew everything and weren't willing to listen to anyone else. Rather than live by the law, they believed they had the right to make their own laws. This same concept has destroyed countless families too.

Take a moment and look around you. Who are the happiest people you know? They're people who work *with* others, not *above* others. They're people who not only offer answers but also ask questions. They are men and women who grow with the times rather than hide from a changing world. The happiest people recognize that they don't know everything and that God didn't make them more special than anyone else. Therefore they are curious, eager to have others teach them, and not afraid to admit either their ignorance or their mistakes. They will open their doors and accept people who look different, think different, and come from different backgrounds.

If you are the sole focus of your thoughts and actions, then you are in the middle of a merry-go-round. You can see the world spinning around you, but you can't focus on the people or situations outside of yourself. Everything is a blur. You have no idea as to what is really going on beyond the point where you stand. Following only your own advice and instincts, you are completely out of touch.

This is true of businesses and churches too. They may say they are marketing their product or their faith to the world, but if their employees or members all are cut from the same piece of cloth, it will be hard for the world to relate to them.

If you want to understand your employees, your friends, your spouse, and your kids, you have to get off the merry-go-round and walk on the ground beside the really important people in your life. This is the only way to see things as they *are*—and seeing that reality is the only way we can make honest decisions that lead to joy and happiness. In other words, you have to join their team and make them a part of yours.

Perhaps it is impossible to go back to the day when President Van Buren caught a cab across town to meet with a young student named Fanny Crosby at the institute for the blind. Yet it was thanks to such visits that the young writer opened the government's eyes to the needs of the handicapped. Thanks to this one-on-one contact, special schools and programs were initiated and millions of those who were once shut away were valued and protected.

Contact is a key in our lives. Think about Jesus—he

could have come back as a powerful king, but instead he chose to walk among the everyday people, listening to their voices and healing their hurts. And he accepted everyone.

There is a wonderful old saying that few use anymore: "Every saint has a past and every sinner has a future." Understanding this is the key to gaining a life in which acceptance is a natural part of your fiber. Hence, we need to get out and meet people eye-to-eye. We need to listen. We need to open our world to others and open our hearts and minds as well. Such openness results in the kinds of opportunities for growth that only come when we include others. If you sit down for dinner with someone who might seem very different from you, you will find you have much more in common than you thought. And that discussion will build a bridge between you two.

You Have to Listen

We get sucked into stubborn pride when we decide we are going to do what we want without getting a second opinion, or when we think we are too wise to seek outside advice. Each time we refuse a helping hand, we sink deeper into the pit of pride.

Once, in the small community of Royal, Illinois, I was part of a band concert. One of the performances spotlighted that night was a trumpet ensemble. As a salute to Americans in uniform, a trio of grade school students was selected to perform.

The problem was that none of the students could agree on which song was to be played first. Rather than give in and find common ground, they bulled forward, none of them accepting the views of the other two. When given the signal to begin, one played the "The Marine's Hymn," another "Anchors Away," and another "The Army Song." To the horror of the school's music teacher, the trio continued to play different numbers throughout their performance. This musical disaster was a product of stubborn pride—and the musicians' pride not only embarrassed them but prevented them from honoring others as they had intended. Stubborn pride sets a fast course for failure at the personal and business level, as it almost always means we are excluding ideas and other people from our lives.

A History Lesson

During World War II, America became a team. With millions fighting the war and millions more at home working to build the machines that would win that war, we were united for a common cause. Rich and poor gave all they could to the war effort. Kids became involved though recycling efforts and war bond drives. Hollywood produced movies that encouraged the nation to work together.

When the war was over, the teamwork remained. People joined civic organizations, churches, and social clubs in numbers that were greater than at any time in our history. Kids became involved in Scouting, organized sports, and youth groups. Americans realized, because of their experiences during the war, that the best way to get things done was through teamwork.

In our modern world, we often stress individualism. Perhaps this is one reason why membership in clubs and churches is down. TV, iPods, and the internet are wonderful tools, but they don't take the place of direct human interaction. We need to experience relationships in person. To be part of a team, we need real, face-to-face, eye-to-eye contact. We can only get that when we join with others striving for a mutual goal. We need to get back to forming and building teams.

Even in our modern world, teamwork is vital. Consider fixing dinner: someone sowed the seed, someone grew the food, someone processed and packaged that food, and so on, all the way until you finally buy it at the store. The next time you think you are a loner who doesn't need people, remember that you need others just to eat!

More important, though, we need people to help us achieve wonderful and lasting things.

Next Steps toward a Grattitude of Teamwork

Write down the teams you are a part of. Begin with your family, and be sure to consider your work, church, school, neighborhood, and so on. You can even go beyond this to your country and the world.

What teams do you contribute to? What friendships

have you formed by being part of a team? List these friends and the gifts they have given you. Consider how your life would be less rich without these friends and their gifts.

Send thank-you notes to acknowledge friends and teammates who have helped you along the way.

What new teams would you like to be part of? What steps do you need to take to join those teams?

A Final Thought

As I learned from Shalee, teamwork is not just about sharing glory; it is also about accepting defeats. When I watched Shalee play, she would often point to herself and say, "My fault," even when it wasn't her error. After a game one night when she had played great but Kansas State lost, she told the reporters, "I need to step it up. I need to play better. I let my team down." In victory Shalee always gave the glory to her teammates. She pointed out plays they made that led to the win. But in defeat she always pointed to something she had not done well enough. In my mind, that defines the perfect teammate and shows why the grattitudes of teamwork and forgiveness must walk hand in hand.

GrATTITUDE

8

SERVICE

More than forty years ago Anne Brooks, a small girl with a shy smile and pigtails, was living in a convent school in Florida. As she raced into the restroom, she was confronted with the sight of Sister Henri Ferdinand — a veteran nun with a quick smile, twinkling eyes, and rosy cheeks — on her hands and knees cleaning a toilet. Anne was shocked. Here was a woman she esteemed above all other women on earth, a woman who had become a mother figure to her, a woman who was her hero — and this powerful woman was doing what Anne believed to be the lowest work there was.

Anne attempted to take the toilet brush from Sister Henri. The girl demanded the nun get up and pass the job to someone who deserved to be doing this kind of disgusting labor. The older woman shook her head and softly explained she was doing this for Anne and that made it the most important job in the world.

It took Anne years to grasp what the nun was attempting

to teach her that day. Yet thirty years later Anne Brooks got down on her knees to provide medical care for the poorest people in the United States. Dr. Anne gave up everything to live and work with the people of the Mississippi Delta. Though her patients have nothing to give her but their thanks and their love, Anne continues to treat their ailments. As a nun once taught her, we cannot hold ourselves above our brothers and sisters and claim that we love them; instead it is the grattitude of service that proves our love.

The Face in the Mirror

Do you remember the children's tale *Snow White*? The witch often looked into her magic mirror and repeated these words: "Mirror, mirror on the wall, who is the fairest of them all?" Each time she spoke, she was sure no one else could come close to matching her beauty; she believed she was the only person in the whole world who mattered.

The witch isn't alone. There are many people who are simply too busy looking at their own reflection in a mirror to ever see anyone else. They live in a universe of one, in which others can be nothing more than servants — and are often less than slaves.

Yet we are called not to stare into mirrors but to look out of windows. When we look out, we discover opportunities to serve, and it is service that really defines happiness and gives us value.

When our vision begins and ends with our image, our

world is a very small place. Mirrors are two-dimensional, and people who spend days looking into them are as well. The world is three-dimensional and is ever changing. It is an exciting and inviting place, but we need to realize that we must take our eyes off the mirror and look out the window.

Tossing Out the Mental Trash

If asked, "Are you more like Jesus or a Pharisee?" most would say, "Jesus." But is that really true in daily life? Are you concerned about image? Are you concerned about hanging out with the right kind of people? Are your values inclusionary or exclusionary? If society were still segregated and the civil rights movement were just beginning, which side would you be on? What stand would you take?

Let's take another look at Christ. By birth he was better than any of us. After all, God was his Father. Yet he lived his whole life not only reaching out to "the least of these" but also living with them. He was a friend to the slave, the sinner, and the common field worker.

Many of his friends, including some of the disciples, didn't get it. They didn't like that Jesus associated with low-lifes. Some, like the Pharisees, were bound and determined to prove themselves better than Jesus. In the beginning days of the church, Jewish members had problems with accepting Gentiles. Even though they had watched Jesus with their own eyes and listened to his message with their own ears, they didn't grasp the full inclusionary message he brought to them.

There is an old Arkansas story about a farmer determined to prove to a mule that he was boss. When the poor animal balked at pulling a wagon, the farmer beat his mule to death. Who lost the one thing that allowed him to make a living? Who was the one the townspeople avoided?

It works the same way with people. If you spend your life constantly trying to lord it over everyone else — beating into them the fact that you are superior — you will be a lonely and angry person, and few will see you as someone of integrity or value. As it says in Philippians 2:5 – 8, our attitude should be the same as that of Christ Jesus, who humbled himself — even to the point of death — and accepted anyone who approached him.

Looking beyond Our Own World

Martin Luther King Jr. knew what it meant to give himself to a cause. Yet in spite of the time spent away from family and friends, and despite being ridiculed and attacked and living a life that gave him little time to pursue his personal desires, he constantly told those around him he was happy. When they asked him to explain how his lifestyle could bring him such joy, he replied, "Life's most urgent question is, what are you doing for others?"

Gayla Whitaker is a friend who exemplifies what King said. She will drop everything to do something for my family when we're in need. When my son was working on a high school film project, she drove more than four hours to help him create costumes. She didn't give up one day—she gave up weeks. She babysits for others on a moment's notice. She helps with charity drives at many churches around town. And the list goes on and on.

Gayla expects nothing in return—not even a thank-you. She constantly reaches out because she wants to help others live their dreams. Her home might be a bit dusty, and her car is never waxed, but that is simply because she is so busy helping everyone else. There are folks who try to take advantage of Gayla, yet no one really can because she treasures giving her life to others. Through Gayla's faithful friendship, I have learned you can't take advantage of someone who freely wants to give you everything you ask—and then give more.

Recently Gayla was struck by pneumonia. The bout was so severe, she was hospitalized and almost lost her life. The hundreds to whom she had given so selflessly over the years now returned the favor. They rushed back to help her. At the time, she was helping a group of college students with a project, and Gayla's friends gave up their vacations to fill in for her. Her service inspired others to serve.

The grattitude of service is contagious; when we serve others, they serve us back—and they serve the world too.

Putting Out Fires or Setting Them?

What happens when we spend all our time looking in the mirror and never look out the window for ways to serve?

Are we happier because we have more time to focus on our own needs and desires? Are we going to see things that need to be fixed around us? Are we going to be reaching out to those in need? If a fire breaks out next door, are we even going to know?

Lucius Domitius Ahenobarbus was born just a few years after Christ was crucified. At the age of sixteen, he succeeded his uncle as the leader of the Roman Empire. History tells us that Lucius — better known as Nero — quickly became enamored with his own knowledge and wisdom. Convinced of his superiority, he discarded his advisors and sought to rule the world according to his own judgments.

Living a lavish lifestyle that put him completely out of touch with the general populace, he failed to understand his own people or the fragile nature of the nation's economic system. Initially popular for assuring Romans that good times would last forever, Nero was increasingly seen as an abject failure, and the economy collapsed. Thus, when the city literally burned around him, the blame was laid on his shoulders.

Like some modern corporate leaders, Nero fiddled as Rome burned. While thousands lost everything they had in the blaze, Nero managed to maintain his exuberant lifestyle. Even after the great fire, his greed and lust seemingly knew no limits. Today he remains a symbol of excess and a cautionary tale about self-absorption.

Although Nero committed suicide in AD 68 — a used-up

man at the age of thirty—his image continues to be seen in our society. During the recent financial crisis, while countless common people lost everything they owned, those responsible for these economic firestorms continued to unashamedly live lifestyles that might have shamed even Nero.

Unfortunately, when such people look in the mirror, they see not a happy face looking back but rather the hollow eyes of greed and continual dissatisfaction. When crisis comes to such people—people who have never served others—there is no one to come serve them.

WWJD?

For several years, the letters WWJD could be seen almost everywhere. WWJD (What Would Jesus Do) was on billboards, notebooks, bumper stickers, T-shirts, and jewelry. Yet what do those letters really mean? Would Jesus spend hours each day looking into a mirror?

On the contrary, Jesus was constantly on the move. He spent time with people where they worked and lived. He was there for their celebrations and their times of mourning. With that in mind, consider for a moment what Jesus would be like in today's world. If Jesus played on a basketball team, he would be thinking of his teammates first, last, and always. If Jesus headed up a large company, he would be out on the production lines finding out what his workers thought and offering them encouraging words. He would be all about service.

During his ministry, Jesus had people pulling at him from all directions. I am sure that each day he had hundreds of requests that included things like, "Jesus, I want you to meet my sister," "Jesus, would you stop by my mother's house? I've told her all about you," "Jesus, would you bless my brother's farm?" and "Jesus, we are having a banquet next week. Could you come?"

In many ways, his life had to have been as crazy as that of a modern celebrity, if not worse. Yet where were his eyes? They weren't looking in a mirror; they were looking out for others.

Thus when he was told about Lazarus, he answered the call. When he found out about the lepers, he went to them. But look deeper at this man's perception. Having a multitude seek him out to hear him speak really points to the fame of the living Jesus. Thousands traveled miles just to reach him. They wanted to hear his thoughts. Yet he was not so caught up in the crowd's fascination with him that he failed to notice their need. They were hungry. So before he spoke, he found a way to feed them. This man's many acts of stopping to touch common people, from calling a tiny man out of a tree to providing a lesson and forgiveness to a woman caught in adultery, all point to one thing—Jesus was always looking outward.

Jesus remains the ultimate role model for every man, woman, and child on earth. During his ministry, it was never about him—it was about us. His life did not show us why *he* was so important to God, but rather his mission was to make us realize *we* were so very important to God.

Egotists are blind, but servants have vision. If egotists fiddle while Rome burns, let us be servants with the love and vision to put out the fires. After all, that is what Jesus did.

Living for Others

Albert Einstein said, "Only a life lived in the service to others is worth living." This is the sort of life that deacons in the church aspire to live, and no one better exemplifies this spirit of servant leadership than Buford Ward. He is a big, smiling man who works a job that is hard and pays little. Buford is also a loving father and husband who lives modestly, drives an older car, and never takes expensive vacations. On the surface, Buford should not stand out—but everyone in Buford's church and community thinks more highly of him than of any rich and famous person.

I was once asked to be a church deacon, and Buford's face instantly popped into my mind. I answered the question with another question: "Thanks, but why don't you talk to Buford Ward?"

"Think about it," I continued. "Who gets up early every Sunday morning and drives the church van? Who goes and visits our members who are in the hospital and nursing home? Who will mow a sick neighbor's grass without being asked? Who plays Santa for the poor kids? Who is there to greet people every time the church doors are open? Who will use his vacation to help with Bible school or church camp? Who never asks for credit for all that he does?"

If those running the nation's biggest companies looked out their windows like Buford always does, they would never have the gall to reward themselves with huge bonuses that could have gone to help others. It is our great challenge to make our actions—and our grattitudes—match WWJD!

Blessings Given Become Blessing Received

When we stare in the mirror, we see only the darkness of our own circumstances. When we look at others, our world becomes full of light and possibility. Often this lesson is taught to us by people whom we might expect to be self-interested and egotistical yet who turn out to be sources of inspiration. The great missionary doctor Albert Schweitzer and the rock legend Bono are not often mentioned in the same breath, yet these men, rather than basking in their own accomplishments, used their talents to save others.

Schweitzer was one of Europe's most gifted musicians. He sold out concerts all over the world. He was also one of the greatest orators of his day. He could have become wealthy as a speaker on the lecture circuit. Yet rather than use these incredible gifts to enrich himself, he used them to fund his missionary work. A self-consumed man would have never said, "If a man loses his reverence for any part of life, he will lose his reverence for all of life." Yet the multitalented

Schweitzer embraced that philosophy. He did so because he looked out his window and saw suffering—and decided to do something about it.

Like Schweitzer, Bono uses his fame and fortune to reach out to the world's poorest people. Bono told some of America's greatest politicians during a National Prayer Breakfast in 2006, "God is in the slums, in the cardboard boxes where the poor play house. God is in the silence of a mother who has infected her child with a virus that will end both their lives. God is in the cries heard under the rubble of war. God is in the debris of wasted opportunity and lives, and God is with us if we are with them." The transcript of his remarks that day has inspired countless sermons and is still read by thousands of people each day.

Schweitzer and Bono chose to live their lives not for themselves but for those they saw suffering around them—and therefore for a humble carpenter who was born in a manger. May we too learn to look away from the mirror and out into the world. Real happiness is found in the bright light of service and friendship. The more we give to the world, the more will be given back to us as we find our place in God's family.

Inspiration at Every Corner

I was recently walking in a city with a college student who was majoring in mass communications. She asked me, "Where do you get all your story ideas?" I pointed to a park bench and we sat down. For the next half hour we didn't speak but rather just looked around at the people of Oklahoma City who were going about a very busy day. Then I signaled it was time to get up and continue our walk.

"What did you see from the bench?" I asked.

"A city in motion," she answered.

"But did you take the time to look at the individual people?"

She shook her head. She really didn't understand what I was saying.

"It's the individual people who are the stories," I explained. "The bus driver who got out of his seat and came off the bus to help the woman with her two children get up the steps. The older man who stopped to pick up someone else's trash and put it in a garbage can. The two people who stopped to help a man who tripped and fell. These are the people who are my inspiration. Why they do what they do is where I find my stories."

I have learned to look around, thanks to people like Dr. Anne Brooks and even Bono. They have embraced the lessons of Christ and have found out that by looking out to others, we grow. The grattitude of service is really a fuel station that always puts more into our tank than we give away to others. If you stop, look, and listen, you will find not only those who inspire you with their small daily doses of grattitudes but also those who need your touch.

Next Steps toward a Grattitude of Service

List friends who give the most to others, and send them a thank-you for their work. That can be your first step toward adding more outreach to your life. Consider partnering with one of those friends in service.

Find projects that fit your interests and your beliefs. You can look for these anywhere. Schools need tutors and mentors. Missions need volunteers. Food pantries need workers. Even local governments use volunteers. Once you identify one group you can serve, sign up. It's best to commit to a regular schedule to ensure you stay involved and can see the fruits of your work over time.

Remember that you often don't have to leave home to serve. Even if you are older or handicapped, making calls to lonely neighbors or friends who are sick, volunteering for your church's prayer line, and sending out cards are ways to serve that can touch people deeply.

If you are in business, list ways you can make service "job number one." Putting the customer first makes financial sense, but it also builds a bond that can be measured in new respect and deep friendship. This includes not only commercial groups but churches too.

A Final Thought

I was watching the news recap the life of Ted Kennedy in the days after his funeral, and a clip was played of a young

Ted when he eulogized his brother Bobby. This would be the third brother that Kennedy had lost in just over three decades of life. When struggling to sum up Bobby's life, Ted spoke of a grattitude we all need to strive for: "My brother need not be idealized, or enlarged in death beyond what he was in life; to be remembered simply as a good and decent man, who saw wrong and tried to right it, saw suffering and tried to heal it, saw war and tried to stop it."

That defines the kind of impact you can have if you put the incredible grattitude of service front and center in your life. If just one person remembers you in that fashion, then you truly have given more to this world than you have taken from it.

GRATTITUDE

9

INTEGRITY

Maybe you've heard the saying "My goal in life is to be as good a person as my dog already thinks I am."

I was speaking to a group in Wisconsin several years ago. After finishing my presentation, I fielded a number of questions. One of the most thought-provoking came from a middle-aged woman with a serious demeanor. "Of all the celebrities you have gotten to know, who is the best role model?"

I didn't hesitate before answering, "Lassie!"

After the laughter died down, I explained. "Lassie loves unconditionally. Lassie is honest to a fault. Lassie will lay down her life for you. Lassie does not judge and is quick to forgive. Lassie always shares. If the world's people were all like Lassie, then life would be pretty wonderful."

Several in the audience began to nod. They realized that when it came to living the grattitude of integrity and having values, Lassie couldn't be beat—few humans come close to measuring up to the canine's high standards. But that shouldn't keep us from trying!

The Need for Integrity

When we live without integrity, people around us are affected. As the old saying goes, "Your life might be the only Bible some read." Imagine you're watching a football game being played in front of fifty thousand fans and a national TV audience. As the ball is set on the tee for the opening kickoff, you are shocked to hear the TV announcer say, "Because these players are all professionals, and because each of them knows the rules, the league has decided there is no need to have officials for the game."

Logically this makes sense. Pro football players know the rules as well as the referees do. They know what constitutes holding, offside, pass interference, and all the other specific rules of the game found in the league handbook.

But logic doesn't always play out in the real world. What would happen without the officials present to enforce the rules of the game? Over time, as people decided to take advantage of the situation, the contest would surely become chaotic. Players would justify bending the rules and then ignore them altogether. Tempers would flare, fights would break out, and the game would become an exercise in futility.

The game of life has rules too. How we play the game defines who we are and the life we live. When we bend the rules, others are hurt, even if we manage to believe we have beaten the system and won the game.

If You Aren't Caught, It's Not Wrong?

Football is played with rules and has people in place to enforce those rules. This is true of life as well. Yet when there is no one watching, do you still follow the rules? Your response to that question says a great deal about your integrity. My grandparents often said, "Character is doing the right thing when no one is looking." I am becoming convinced that those eleven words should be chiseled in stone in every public building in the country.

Several years ago I was having supper with a large group of individuals I barely knew. In the course of the conversation, the subject of the April 15 tax-filing date came up. Many of us were lamenting that we had yet to begin to fill out our annual tax statements. In the midst of our excuses as to why we had not yet filed, a man piped up and said, "I never worry about that."

We were all amazed by the calm fashion in which the gentleman viewed this ominous date. One of my friends, a banker, asked the guest his secret. With a smile, the man replied, "I haven't paid any taxes in more than twenty years." He then added that he didn't pay any Social Security either.

You could have heard a pin drop in the room as we all stared at the smug stranger. As the evening continued, we found out his secret. He only accepted payment to his business in cash, never reported any income, and therefore had stayed under the Internal Revenue Service's radar for two decades.

Since that evening I have listened to others, many of whom were very wealthy, brag about the ways they cheated the federal, state, and local governments. Many of their schemes were technically legal, but their moral status was clear. While these people seemed proud of beating the government, I knew that my grandfather would have been disgusted.

Those serving in our military were being cheated by those who balked at paying their fair share, as were schools, hospitals, and even the highway system.

What is more appalling than the cheats themselves is the fact that many taxpayers actually envy them. I have heard several folks say, "I wish I had that guy's guts" or "I wish had that person's lawyers and accountants." Yet it is just as morally impossible to justify stealing from the government as it is to justify stealing from another person. In each instance, an individual is not only breaking one of the Ten Commandments but also disregarding the instructions given by Christ to render unto Caesar what is Caesar's. On April 15, as well as every other day of the year, we need to play by the rules.

So far this tax cheat seems to have escaped the consequences of disobeying the law of the United States. Yet what if his actions inspire someone else to cheat, and that person gets caught? What if this man needs help from the system at some point? And even if he is never caught, what will he say when he has to justify his actions before God?

Honesty's Legacy

My father regularly reminded me that my name stood for honor and integrity. He hoped and prayed that I would not just recognize that legacy but also embrace it. I tried my best to follow his desires, but it wasn't until the age of fifty-five that I realized just how dynamic and long-lasting that legacy could be.

My wife and I were visiting a homecoming celebration at our youngest son's school, Ouachita Baptist University, in Arkadelphia, Arkansas. One of the gentlemen I met was from the Ozark Mountain community of Batesville, Arkansas. My father went to college in that city, and I had visited it many times over the years. I began to ask him about how Batesville had changed since I was last there. In the course of hearing his great stories, I happened to mention the name of my mother's father.

At that point the stories stopped.

My grandfather, Tom Shell, was not a famous man. He was simply a small-town businessman who called Salem, Arkansas, home. Yet, as I was soon to find out, his reputation went far behind the community where he lived and died.

I knew my grandfather to be honest to a fault. He always played by the rules. He never overcharged anyone. The work he did for others was of even higher quality than the work he would do for himself. His word was as close to a guarantee as is humanly possible. As someone said at his funeral, "If Tom Shell said it, you could take it to the bank."

The man I met that day had been told about *my* grandfather by *his* grandfather. He had even been proudly introduced to my grandfather when he was a child. He had heard the stories of how my grandfather represented the type of honesty that everyone should adhere to. Because I was his grandson, I was immediately seen as possessing those same qualities—and so were my sons!

Imagine a fourth generation benefiting from a life lived with consistent integrity! More than a decade after my grandfather's death, and more than two hundred miles from the place where he'd lived his life, *my* status as a human suddenly grew richer in the eyes of a stranger simply because of Grandpa's integrity.

Is Honesty the Best Policy?

Today I see a lot of folks who believe that playing by the rules is a sign of weakness. Honesty, for them, is *not* the best policy. Their faces can be seen all over the front pages of newspapers and on our televisions. For many, beating the rules seems to be more important than earning respect. In business, sports, and even education, those who disregard the rules and benefit from doing so have created a universe where integrity seems to be as outdated as a Model T.

I was raised a different way.

Once I was coming back from Waco, Texas, and stopped at an ice cream parlor. I bought a cone, gave the cashier a ten-dollar bill, grabbed the change, and drove the thirty-two miles home. There I noticed that the young man working the counter had given me change for a twenty. Looking at the extra money, I thought, "I hit the jackpot!"

However, that lucky feeling lasted only a few short seconds. As I pulled the extra ten out and studied it, I remembered my father's words and my grandfather's example. It was already past nine, so going back to Waco would mean I would lose another hour or more out of what had already been a long day—not to mention the price of the gas to make the trip. Besides, this was not my mistake.

Yet because of the value my family and I always placed on living with integrity, I swallowed my rationalizations, got back in the car, and hit the road.

Half an hour later, the kid working the counter was overjoyed—he would have had to make up the shortage in the cash drawer out of his own pocket. I won't say I was overjoyed—I was too tired for that—but I was happy that I'd done the right thing.

When you are living a life of gratitudes, the right policy *is* the best policy.

We Reap What We Sow

There is an old gospel song called "Run On." Who wrote this classic number is unknown, but the song's lyrics clearly illustrate that when you play by your own rules, there are always consequences.

You may throw your rock and hide your hand
Working in the dark against your fellow man
As sure as God made the day and the night
What you do in the dark will be brought to the light
You may run and hide, slip and slide
Trying to take the mote from your neighbor's eyes
As sure as God made the rich and poor
You gonna reap just what you sow.

Barry Bonds and several famous baseball stars became legends and broke records by using performance-enhancing drugs. The usual response of these players when they were finally caught was stark silence or "Well, everyone else was doing it."

Before they were caught, these top names in sports made millions and basked in the rays of fame. Yet when their deception was revealed, they tried to run from the spotlight and hide in the darkness. Their actions dramatically hurt the popularity of their sport and influenced millions with the immoral claim that it's okay to cheat if you don't get caught.

What they failed to grasp is that having integrity—doing the right thing even when no one is watching—is the only way to gain lasting respect and goodness. As quickly as these cheaters rose in fame, they plummeted back to earth, and it will take a lifetime for them to regain any sense of honesty.

The grattitude of integrity can't be checked at the door—we wear it 24/7.

The Scoreboard

Integrity is about more than just being right all the time—it is also about immediately correcting yourself when you realize that you have made a mistake.

I officiated basketball games for fourteen years. I was a good official who knew the rules and generally made solid decisions. Yet there were times when I messed up. There were moments in the heat of the game when I blew the whistle and gave the ball to the wrong team or called a foul on the wrong player.

Whenever possible, I immediately overruled my own call. That was a humbling experience, since it meant I had to stop the game, huddle with the other officials, then walk over to the scorer's table and explain to the person in charge of the books and to the two coaches that I had messed up. However, it was important to assure that the game would not be determined by a mistake I could correct. My looking a bit stupid was not nearly as important as a fair game for the players and fans.

The key in my admission was timing. It would have done no good to admit my mistake after the game had already ended. A person of integrity steps forward as soon as they realize they were wrong. Putting it off only puts you in a deeper hole, and it compromises your values in the eyes of others.

A Girl Named Mary

James Miles won the Congressional Medal of Honor for heroic action during the Civil War. To survive that cataclysmic American tragedy took not only incredible bravery but also the help of many who were not recognized for their actions. Miles was one of the first freed black men to serve his country in the Civil War. Well-spoken and cultured, he was placed in charge of men who had never held a gun, knew nothing about fighting, and had no formal education. In a sense, he was given the soldiers others did not want. Yet he treated these unskilled men with the same respect he did careeer military officers. In the Battle of Caffin's Farm, he led his men, providing confidence and assurance, even after having his left arm mutilated by shrapnel. Bleeding profusely from an injury so bad that later he had to have his arm amputated, he raced into enemy fire to protect those in his band who had become to scared to fight. When he was later asked why he risked his life in such a way, he replied, "You can easily judge the character of a man by how he treats those who can do nothing for him."

When I was a freshman in high school, in the days before mentally disabled kids were mainstreamed into regular classrooms, I was appalled at the way many of my friends treated the students in special education classes. I remember one girl in particular. Mary was homely, heavy, and very trusting. Boys in my class took great delight in toying with her emotions and innocence. They lied to her about the way they felt about her. At times they made her believe she was their girlfriend. When she was walking on air, they broke her heart and made her cry. As tears flowed down her cheeks, they laughed. Why did they torture her? Because they wanted to feel like they were superior. They wanted to feel as if they had power over someone else.

When I questioned them, their answer was always, "She's too stupid to know what's going on. It's just a game. It's fun. No one is getting hurt." None of those statements was true. It was all about values, and as Miles noted, integrity or the lack thereof can be best seen by how we treat those who we think don't matter.

Another way to view this is from a biblical perspective. If you turn to Matthew 25:35 – 40, you will find Christ talking about people who touched him when they reached out to those who were hungry, naked, sick, or in prison. Thus the grattitude of integrity really begins with how we look at others. If we find ways to elevate ourselves above others because of skin color, social standing, education, or financial status, then we are already lacking in the kind of integrity that the Bible endorses. This grattitude doesn't just embrace telling the truth; it also involves the way we treat others.

Next Steps toward a Grattitude of Integrity

List five people who you believe have great integrity, and write down the character traits they have that contribute to their integrity. Consider any traits that reoccur and that you would like to make part of your own grattitudes.

Imprint those traits in your life by listing places where you can use them. An example would be not cutting corners on a job, or always telling the truth to your kids. Become detail oriented and give your friends or customers more than they expect.

Make a list of people who look up to you. If you can, put photos of these people where you can easily see them. Whenever you are tempted to bend your principles, look into the faces in those photos, and remember that integrity is a legacy that can stretch across generations.

A Final Thought

Mary was an easy target for the boys at my school. But as we conclude our look at integrity, let's go back to the beginning of this chapter and revisit our first role model for integrity. How would Lassie have reacted to Mary? The dog would have shown her the same kind of love that she showed everyone else. In fact, Lassie would have stepped between Mary and her tormentors. The dog would have protected her. How we would respond to someone in Mary's situation says a great deal about our integrity.

GrATTITUDE
10

LOVE

Keith Willhite was a vibrant man in his early forties when he received the news that he had terminal brain cancer. To the father of a girl who was about to become a teenager and a son who was still in elementary school, the medical verdict was devastating.

As he shared the news with his wife, the homiletics professor at Dallas Theological Seminary was overwhelmed by all of the future family events he would be missing. More than just mourning his personal losses, he felt he was letting his family down.

Many trapped in Keith's situation would have drawn into a shell and attempted to push people out of their lives, hoping to avoid some of the emotional pain. Yet through his faith Keith knew the incredible power of love. He realized that love freely given would not die, even if his heart stopped beating.

But how do you give love when you are no longer there to wrap and deliver that precious gift?

For Keith, the answer was as close as his desk. With careful consideration and deliberate thought, he began to compose letters to his children, to be given at each significant stage in their lives. In these letters, he penned important stories, shared special memories, wrote bits and pieces of humor and inspiration, and, most of all, inscribed words that presented his undying love.

Keith died when Katie was thirteen. When she got her driver's license, her mother handed her a letter her father had written that expressed his pride and excitement. When Katie had her first date, a letter provided her with her father's wisdom on growth. When Katie graduated from high school, she received another letter filled with congratulations and a father's pride.

Keith's love, which had meant so much to Katie when he was alive, still surrounds her. There are more letters waiting for future events such as her college graduation, her wedding day, and the birth of her children. In fact, there are even letters written for Katie's future kids.

Keith Willhite fully understood what many do not — life's greatest grattitude is love, and love does not die.

What Is Love?

Each grattitude in this book is important to building character and embracing the fullness of a life well lived, but none has the deep and lasting impact of love. In fact, love is the one grattitude that will guide us to embrace the other nine.

It is written in 1 Corinthians 13:4–8 that "love is patient, love is kind. It does not envy, it does not boast, it is not proud. It is not rude, it is not self-seeking, it is not easily angered, it keeps no record of wrongs. Love does not delight in evil but rejoices with the truth. It always protects, always trusts, always hopes, always perseveres. Love never fails."

Love Sustains

I have been blessed to receive much love in my life, but one example stands above the rest. My wife has given me unconditional love for more than three decades. She has never withheld her love, even in the toughest of times when we were wondering where our next paycheck would come from. When I was struggling to make it as a writer, she told me, "You can walk on water as long as you don't look down. Keep your eye on the prize and don't sink. I believe in you." That belief was fueled by love.

As her friends built dream houses and drove new cars, she didn't once complain or tell me, "I'm tired of your dream. Get a real job." She just kept cheering for me. Kathy has been there through sickness and health and in bad times and good.

I have to look no further than Kathy to find my example of unconditional love. Yet it goes beyond me. She shows it to her family, her friends, to those at church and at her job, and even to the neighborhood stray cats. She gives her love freely, and her love knows no boundaries.

When I consider how much she has given up to support me, I pledge to embrace the greatest of God's gifts by trying my best to reflect Kathy's love to her and to all those I meet. Love is the greatest gift and the precondition to putting all the other grattitudes into action. Love is the ultimate blessing and, simply put, you can't have too much of it in your life.

Compassion

Love is more than what happens in a family. Love, or the lack of it, is seen in every action we take. Perhaps the purest form of love can be witnessed when someone reaches out in compassion to a stranger.

This kind of selfless love can even be seen on a college softball field. In April 2008, Western Oregon was playing Central Washington in a college softball game in the small community of Ellensburg, Washington. Few were in the stands to witness what some could call a crowning moment in sportsmanship.

In a 0-0 game with two runners on base, Western Oregon's Sara Tucholsky, a five-foot-two senior who rarely played and had only had three hits all season, got ahold of a pitch and drove it out of the park. It was her first career home run. The excited Sara was at first base when her leg gave out. In a freak accident, she stepped on the bag wrong, tearing ligaments in her knee. The stadium went silent as she fell to the ground, screaming in pain.

The game stopped as trainers came out to attend to the young woman. It was quickly apparent that she was not going to be able to continue her trek around the bases. Pulling out the rulebook, the head umpire explained that since Sara had only reached first base, her home run would become a single. Because of her injury, Sara would not get credit for the only home run she had ever hit—and it was pretty obvious that her knee injury meant she might not ever play again.

Just as Sara's coach prepared to send a substitute runner out to first base, Central Washington's senior shortstop stepped into the picture. Mallory Holtman, who was her school's record holder in home runs, asked the umpires, "Excuse me, would it be okay if I carried her around the bases and she touched each bag? Then would the home run count?"

As the umpires consulted the rulebook, Mallory, who had suffered several knee injuries and would be going back for another surgery after the season, waited for their ruling. At last the officials gave the okay, and Mallory picked up the injured Sara and carried her the rest of the way around the bases. Accompanied by a standing ovation, the pair made it to home plate, where Mallory lifted Sara into the arms of her own Oregon teammates.

When later asked about her act of love, Mallory shrugged and said she was simply doing what she believed anyone would do if they were faced with a similar situation.

In truth, few of us would choose to put ourselves second in the way Mallory did that day. But love always puts the needs of others first. On a Washington softball field, an act of selflessness gave the world a lesson in love.

A Cat's Tale

A decade ago someone dropped a black-and-white kitten on our front porch. As we already had one cat in our home, we really didn't want another, but we simply couldn't let the orphaned kitten die, and she was too young to fend for herself. Within a few hours Buffy had a home.

Six years ago a beaten-up, yellow tomcat appeared in our yard. He was a true feral cat, the product of a mother who had survived on her own. He was tough and self-sufficient and had the scars to prove it. At one point in his life he had been in some type of fight or accident, and three inches of his tail were missing. We called him Short-Tail. We started leaving food for Short-Tail in hopes he would hang around. He quickly came to realize that at 5:30 each evening a cup of Special Kitty cat food would be placed in a bowl just for him.

Short-Tail began to stick closer and closer to our house. This once wild and wary cat actually began to allow us to pet him. Over the course of three years, he transformed. Now whenever anyone from our family drives up to the house, he races out to meet them. I have never known an animal or a human who so treasures the kind touch of a hand and who is so grateful for the food he is given each day. With his purrs, the expression on his face, and his body language, he is constantly saying, "Thank you."

Short-Tail grew up in the wild. With no one catering to his needs, he was smart enough to realize that if he was going to make it, he would have to work hard. His instincts and experience must have told him that life didn't owe him anything but a chance to live one more day. Thus when we give him food and love on him, I think he sees it for what it is—a gift. And judging by the way he treats us, I believe that gift is something he never takes for granted.

Meanwhile Buffy rarely acknowledges we are alive. When we walk in the door, she usually sleeps through it. If we pet her, she acts as though she is doing us a favor. The only time she pays any attention to us is when her food bowl is empty, she has a hairball that needs to be taken out, or her litter box needs cleaning. Buffy has the "you owe me" attitude, while Short-Tail has the "thank you so much for caring about me" attitude. We can't embrace the gifts of love if we have a selfish attitude. I would even go so far as to argue that selfishness is the straightest path to spiritual failure. It leads to an isolated life with very little love and creates a world where enough is never enough. As long as we hold on to this attitude, we can never be a real role model to those who love us. And, unlike Short-Tail, we will never realize the blessings that surround us each day, or feel regular touches from a loving and compassionate hand.

Put another way, we are closest to God when we are following in Jesus' footsteps—and Jesus never supposed that anyone owed him anything. Instead he gave himself as a gift for all.

Giving one's life is the ultimate act of love.

Loveless and Lonely

My oldest son, Clint, is surviving tough economic times by using his college degree to wait tables. In fact, the entire wait staff at the restaurant where he works has at least a four-year degree. Recently a well-known businessman was seated at one of Clint's tables and ordered a steak. A family at the next table ordered just after the businessman did. When the family received their quick-to-prepare meal before the businessman got his specially prepared steak, he became enraged. He cussed out my son for slighting him, explaining that he was special and his status demanded that he receive his meal before a common tourist was served. After threatening to have my son fired, he threw down his napkin and stormed out without paying. As the waiter in charge, Clint had to fork over the money for the expensive meal that was never eaten.

Our feral cat Short-Tail has more character in one whisker than this businessman has in his entire three-piece suit.

Thankfully for my son, a happier lesson was provided. A couple who had witnessed what happened called Clint over and told him not to worry about the rude customer. They assured him that he was not at fault. Their words brought my son some comfort, but it was their gift that saved his day. When they left, they not only gave a generous tip but also paid the man's bill. That was love in action!

The world is full of people who demand service and respect but are never grateful. They are always looking for ways to get what they want before even considering other people. It is in working and serving that true satisfaction is realized.

Love seeks ways to right wrongs. My son had a wrong righted by someone who had love in their hearts and let it out. In this way, there is a close tie between love and justice.

Just Saying It

For some, it is easy to say, "I love football," "I love shopping," "I love Texas," or "I love my car." Yet when it comes time for these same people to say, "I love you," the words get caught in their throat. When fall weekends roll around, it is obvious when someone loves football. Not only do they cry out from the rooftops, but they literally live for the games. They tune in to TV, they follow on the internet, and some even wear team gear during the contests.

Yet put those same people in front of a friend or a family member, and they often have to be forced into saying those words and flaunting that emotion. They look at the ground and say something like, "You know I love you. I don't have to say it." If we have no problem saying we love football, then why do we have issues with saying we love our spouse, offspring, or friends?

For years our society has seemed to teach that openly showing love for others is a sign of weakness. In truth, it is just the opposite. It is a display of strength. Those who are the most confident are those who have no problem saying, "I love you." So take the enthusiasm you have for things you love and translate it to those you love, and love will bloom like spring flowers in your life.

What Is Real Love?

Love is compassion put into action. It is putting yourself second and everyone else first. It is rejecting selfishness and embracing service. It is picking up someone who has fallen and carrying them back home. It is realizing that our words and actions go beyond the span of our lives—and ensuring that we leave the gift of love for those we love.

I had a friend who was approached by a small, hungry child in a slum in Kenya. My friend knew he needed to do something for the child, so he reached into his pocket and retrieved a candy bar. The child eagerly took it and ate it. A Kenyan policeman asked the American, "Why did you do that? It is a waste. The boy will be hungry again tomorrow, and you won't be here to feed him."

My friend replied, "I did it because I should love this child as my own. But you are right, I won't be here tomorrow." That truth troubled my friend, so over the next few months he met with scores of Americans and Kenyans and formed a school in the midst of the slum. The school educated and fed hundreds of children, including the little boy on the street. One act of love kicked off a mission that has now touched thousands.

If you love, you don't keep score. There will always be those who have more than you do, as well as those who have less. Love isn't about keeping up with the Joneses. Love is about being thankful for all blessings—large and small—and always giving back.

I was visiting with my Grandmother Collins about thirty years ago. This woman was in her eighties and had never really had anything. She had never even owned a car, and she lived in a tiny home that most would consider pretty low-rent. When I asked her about having worked so hard and possessing so little, she laughed and pointed to a suitcase filled with snapshots.

"My wealth is in my memories," she told me. "My bank account is filled with love. I wouldn't trade those for all the money on earth."

When I pointed out that the folks up the street had a big house or vacationed in Europe, she smiled and said, "Hope they're as happy as I am."

That's the way love is. It measures success in relationships, not dollars.

Love reminds us that we are no better than anyone else. This also means that in God's eyes, no one is better than you. When you have love in your heart, you don't usually worry about being owed.

Love is the great equalizer. It provides us with a bridge that connects us with others rather than tearing us apart. It is the grattitude that causes us to act and expect nothing in return for our actions.

For more than thirty years in Dallas, Texas, a woman has cooked Thanksgiving dinner for hundreds of homeless people. She doesn't turn away anyone who comes to her home. She doesn't ask them why they are on the streets, if they are addicts, or if they have criminal records. She just feeds them and embraces them with her strong, loving arms.

Why does she do it? She told a local television station she feels blessed to have a family and a home. She is surrounded by those who care about her. Therefore she is driven to make sure that those on the streets know that someone cares for them as well. This is love in action.

Love allows us to freely work with people and not to put them under our thumbs. Thanks to love, we want to be part of a team, not a drag on it.

Few performers love their fans, and I do mean love, like the Oak Ridge Boys. This country music group has been traveling the country for more than four decades, and at each stop they spend hours shaking hands, posing for pictures, and signing autographs. They even answer emails and keep folks tuned in to their daily schedules on Facebook. Why do they spend all these hours? Their lead singer,

Duane Allen, told me, "They are a part of our team. In fact, they are our bosses. We owe them for all their support."

Recognizing who has helped make you successful is the first step in really seeing the members of your team. The next step is making sure they know how important you think they are. When you share that grattitude, you are displaying love.

The Oak Ridge Boys fully understand that if you embrace love and share it, then each day of life is a blessing. Each day is a day to tell someone you love them and make sure they know it is real. This is what families, churches, and businesses need to embrace as well.

Real love is presented so freely that it literally flows from your heart.

Why does a rich rocker like Bono give away millions of dollars and months of his time to the poorest of the poor? He will tell you that his love of his God demands that he do it. Love inspires us to do good works. In fact, if love is bubbling over in your heart, you can't help but get involved in helping those who are unloved. Love causes us to look out and not look in.

Love is the one commodity we can possess that is replenished and increased when it is given away.

When we tell someone we love them, they almost always respond with an act of love. In a very real sense, you can't give love away. It always comes back. In India more than five decades ago John Douglas took in seven orphans. He showed his love to them and cared for them. The word got out. Soon others he had touched with his love asked if they could help him care for the kids. With this new support, Douglas returned to India and took in more street orphans. Within ten years, he had established more than one hundred children's homes, and had plans for many more. The momentum of the organization's growth could be matched only by the great need to reach even more children. Almost three decades later an Indian newspaper declared upon the man's death, "John Douglas, Father of a Million Children, Has Died."

Love works best when all the other grattitudes are in place and are a natural part of your life. Love is the sum total of every grattitude in this book. Love comes easily and fully when we embrace self-discipline, growth, courage, humor, tenacity, forgiveness, teamwork, service, and integrity.

Next Steps toward a Grattitude of Love

List those you love. Decide how you will let them know you love them, and think about how you could love them more than you already do.

List your love heroes, the people who best model godly love. What about them shows their love so well? Think about how you can emulate those role models to display even more love to those around you. Go beyond your family to your neighbors, business partner, and customers.

List the last time you told those close to you how much

you love them, then vow to tell them more often. Don't keep your loved ones guessing as to how you feel. Tell them.

List the things you have in your life that are due to someone's gifts of love, and thank those who loved you enough to give you those gifts.

Set up a journal of love. Every time someone shows or tells you they love you, write it down. When you realize how often love is expressed to you, you'll be encouraged to show even more love in your words and actions.

A Final Thought

As an only child, I was never blessed with a sister or brother. I was in my twenties when a wonderful woman named Louise Mandrell demanded the role as my "adopted" sister — and now she is like an aunt to my kids and a sister to my wife. Louise and I still talk often on the phone, and her parting words — no matter what we talk about or what we're feeling — are always, "I love you."

Don't hesitate to say these words. Let them pass your lips as freely as the air you breathe. Make sure those you love are assured of your love verbally. To Keith Willhite, those three words were so powerful that he wrote them in letters to be read after he died.

In 1 Corinthians 13, Paul lists a number of wonderful grattitudes, but he ends that section of his writing with this short commentary: "The greatest of these is love." You can take that grattitude to the bank!

Conclusion

Attitude or Grattitude?

Webster defines attitude this way: "a manner, disposition, feeling, position, etc., with regard to a person or thing."

Now, as we wind down this book, let's view attitude in a way we often look at it these days. When a teacher or coach says, "He's got an attitude," it is not a positive remark. In this sense, having an attitude is not a good thing.

Attitude

"Attituders" are complainers. They yell and moan about what is wrong and don't get anything done. Attituders seem to revel in making everyone miserable. And you don't have to look very far to find them.

Attituders can be heard almost any time of the day on talk radio. They often scream and find great fault in things the other side is doing. They almost always feel like someone is out to get them, and forgiveness is not something that they embrace. They point out problems but don't outline solutions. In fact, attituders don't listen; they are too busy trying to make their point, which they believe is the only one worth having.

It was the attituders who led the march to crucify Jesus, supported Hitler, and tried to stop America's integration.

Grattitude

Webster defines gratitude as "the quality or feeling of being grateful or thankful." It then states that gratitude is "the essence of good mental health and spirituality." Now, people with this quality sound like folks we would have to have over for dinner.

"Grattituders" are those who see their blessings, look for solutions, lift up rather than put down, and solve problems. Grattituders make life better for everyone around them because they care deeply about more than just themselves.

In other words, grattituders are doers. You may not hear them, they won't be yelling on street corners or screaming during radio broadcasts, but you can see their work. They are spiritual healers whose touch can bring comfort and understanding. They encourage and don't judge. They don't set themselves apart from others; instead they see all people as their brothers and sisters.

Your Choice

Each of us has a choice. We choose the team we want to be on. The choice you have to make is whether you want to be an attituder or a grattituder. If you decide to be like those who have brought light into a dark world, then you will be a grattituder, and the world will be a better place because of your choice.

The following are sample
chapters from *Sticks and Stones:
Using Your Words as a Positive Force*,
by Ace Collins

Introduction

Words Can Never Harm Me

One of the most familiar of childhood sayings is, "Sticks and stones can break my bones, but words can never harm me." If only that were true! Words have derailed political campaigns, started wars, ruined marriages, and even led to a man named Jesus being crucified on the cross. The fact is, words are a powerful tool and perhaps an even more powerful weapon. They can destroy and they can inspire. And how we use them says a great deal about each of us.

As a writer I have had the privilege of interviewing some of the most incredible people in the world. Their words and stories have made a profound impact on my life. Yet I have not had the opportunity to share many of the lessons I've learned from these experiences with anyone but my family and friends. What I have learned has so changed the way I view the power of words that I felt a need to share these lessons in the very medium that I have come to realize has so much power—a book.

Consider this: Ron Ballard was paralyzed from the neck down after a car wreck. He was confined to a single room in his parents' home. He should have been forgotten, but one Sunday-school teacher's words not only kept him alive but also gave him the faith and drive to start a movement that changed the world for tens of millions of other disabled people.

Or how about this: Gene Mauldin was always told he would amount to nothing. He heard it so much that he believed every word. Only after he was blinded during the Vietnam War did someone finally tell him how much talent he had been given. He took that belief and became an honors student in college and eventually one of St. Louis's top homebuilders. Words allowed him to see his potential even after he lost his sight.

I felt I needed to share these and scores of other stories. Putting this book together became a mission that simply would not let me go. You are holding in your hand the essence of what I believe is a formula for combating an increasingly negative world. In these pages are examples of how thinking before we speak or write can open up new horizons for those around us. And with your positive influence, those you touch will touch others, and the world will become a brighter place. We need that light in this century filled with so many fears and uncertainties.

In his play *Richelieu; Or the Conspiracy*, Edward Bulwer-Lytton wrote the famous line, "The pen is mightier than the sword." How true. When properly used, words, both written and spoken, can make a greater and longer-lasting impact than the most powerful weapons ever constructed. Yet in a time when the average person employs thirty thousand words daily through conversation and correspondence, most of our words miss a great deal more often than they hit, and those that hit often cause pain, not healing.

Properly used, language can and should have a positive impact. Words should cause people to stop, think, and grow. They should bring comfort, cheer, and inspiration. They should change the world by influencing individuals in a positive manner. While what we say or write might never be quoted like Lincoln's "Gettysburg Address" or Paul's love passage in 1 Corinthians 13, with just a little thought and effort, each of us can cause our family, friends, co-workers, and even complete strangers to try to meet their highest goals or to reach down to lift another up.

We live in an era when language is simply tossed about in an unthinking manner or spun to fit an agenda. Though we as individuals talk a great deal in person and on cell phones and, thanks to the internet, write more personal and business notes than any previous generation, we don't as carefully consider our choice of words as did people of earlier times. Most of us, including parents, church leaders, CEOs, coaches, and friends, just "shoot from the hip" and do far more damage with our words than we realize. While a word or phrase more carefully chosen might have inspired someone, what we see much more often today is the use of words that hurt and destroy individuals.

Using real-life examples, this book presents simple ways in which everyone can make a positive impact with their language. Whether it's in conversations, email, letters, phone calls, thank-yous, and even blogging, you will discover ways to employ words that will change the world. There is nothing revolutionary in this book, just written reminders put together in formulas that might help you make words a positive force in what has become a very negative world. If you want to make those thirty thousand words you use each day count, then this book will help you get more out of the time you spend communicating with others each and every day.

1

Talking to Yourself

A few years ago I was watching a high-school girls' basketball game in a small town in Texas. It was an exciting contest, with parents cheering for the kids, coaches yelling out instructions, and players using their talents to try to score points on one end of the gym and stop their opponents on the other.

The point guard for the Bynum Lady Bulldogs was a cute, small brunette named Brittany. The fifteen-year-old was doing her best to bring the ball up the floor against a suffocating full-court press. Moving to her right, Brittany dribbled up the sideline, only to be confronted by a double-team and to have the ball bounced against her knee and out of bounds. After the whistle blew, there was a moment of almost churchlike silence in the building. Then Brittany cried out, "Oh, Brittany!"

Brittany was obviously upset with her play. Her words, meant to be heard by no one other than herself, indicated her frustration even more than the look on her face did. As the game continued, I noted that she continued to whisper words of encouragement and exclamations of frustration to herself for the rest of the night. In fact, I found her one-sided conversation to be the most interesting part of the game.

Like Brittany, we all talk to ourselves. It's part of our nature. Contrary to popular opinion, we aren't crazy just because we ask ourselves questions and then provide a few answers. Many of us might not voice our thoughts, but I don't know of anyone who doesn't internalize conversations. What we say to ourselves varies from day to day and situation to situation, but how we say it affects not only our choices in life but how we relate to the rest of the world. If our own words label us as losers, then we usually live down to that status.

I Think I Can!

One of the best-loved children's stories is about a small locomotive trying to pull a big load up a mountain. While we might not remember the details of the story, the tiny engine's words are probably still etched in everyone's mind: "I think I can, I think I can, I think I can!" Using that philosophy, the tiny locomotive steamed over the mountain and then proudly told itself, "I knew I could!"

For many, though, the voice we hear on the inside more often than not says, "You can't do that." And if those are the words you hear each day, then you probably aren't able to say much that is encouraging to anyone else either.

An old axiom says you really can't like others unless you like yourself. This can be expanded to include another significant rule: you really can't say much to motivate others in a positive way if you are drowning in doubts and negativity.

t e t   pen n

One of the reasons I enjoy watching kids play basketball is that I played all through grade school and high school. In fact, I still like to get out on the court today. In addition, my father was an incredible coach who excelled at teaching fundamental skills. Several of his players went on to play at major colleges.

Dad taught us how to shoot free throws. He went into every nuance, including fingertip control, stance, and release. Yet even though he could teach the proper technique to every kid, certain individuals simply couldn't consistently hit free throws. The problem wasn't with their form; it was in their head. They always went up to the line convinced they were going to miss the shot. They couldn't latch on to my dad's best piece of advice: "Picture it going through the goal before you release the ball." Instead, the picture in their minds was of the ball clanking on the rim and falling off to the side. Rather than having an "I know I can make it" attitude, they said to themselves words like, "I'm going to miss it."

Even when everything is going right in your life, even when you have the skills, the experience, and the tools to accomplish something, if you are telling yourself, "I am going to mess this up," you probably will. The words you speak to yourself are probably the most important words you will ever say.

Breaking the Mold

Several weeks ago I read the story of Nola Ochs. In May 2007 she graduated with honors from Fort Hays State University in Hays, Kansas. As the history major received her degree, everyone, including the governor of the state, stood and applauded. Her blue eyes glowing, the small woman grinned, took her diploma, and moved across the stage and back to her seat. The ever-modest Nola considered herself to be just another student and didn't want to steal the spotlight from any of her many friends in the class of 2007. Yet the fact that she was ninety-five years old did cast her in a much different light than her classmates.

As middle age begins to throw its arms around us, our internal voice tells us to slow down and give up on our dreams. The voice inside our head that once pushed us to try to change the world now screams, "You can't do that now; you are simply too old." This voice usually becomes louder as we hit our senior years. Rather than think with the old "I think I can" mentality, we tend to say, "I wish I could," or even worse, "There's no way."

Nola never allowed her mind to convince her body that she couldn't do anything she dreamed of doing. She had run a large family farm after her husband died. She had driven tractors, bailed hay, and taken crops to the market. She had raised livestock. All the while, the voice in her head kept saying, "You know you can do it." When most members of her high school class were holding their reunions at the cemetery, Nola took some courses at a community college and then at the age of ninety-four moved to the campus at Fort Hays State to become a coed. She donned the colors of the Fort Hays State Tigers at the same time as her granddaughter did.

Nola's work ethic, self-discipline, and drive inspired her professors and other students, who were often seven decades her junior. As they got to know Nola, they were transformed simply by watching her positive approach to life. Her can-do spirit pulled a lot of self-doubters to heights they never believed they could achieve. Students who were tempted to skip classes or put off homework got out of bed and went to work because of the white-haired student who greeted each challenge with a big smile and an even bigger can-do attitude.

One of the keys to Nola's success was very simple; Nola liked herself. She felt she had value and worth. She was confident enough to walk into a situation in which she would stand out, in which most people expected her to fail or fall behind. Each day, she got up believing she could handle whatever life threw at her. She even felt it was a joy to meet those challenges.

Her work ethic, the premium she put on learning, her quest to embrace fully every moment of her life, and her positive attitude made a huge impact on her fellow students. The kids who went to school with her saw firsthand that there was nothing that could hold them back or stand in their way except their own attitudes. When they watched Nola gain her degree, they understood that with hard work and the right can-do spirit, they too could realize the fullness of a life that has no boundaries.

oo n   e

For every Nola there are tens of thousands of people of all ages who simply believe they are too old, too short, too slow, too thin, too fat, or just too something to do anything. Hence they don't even start to do what they really want to do. The voice inside their head is a "can't-do attitude." They are constantly explaining to themselves and to others that what they wish for can never be realized because of something that is holding them back. The words they speak to themselves are excuses rather than challenges.

The attitude expressed by the words "I just can't do it" not only holds people back in their own lives but also is passed on to others. If someone close to you has this attitude, it can affect you as deeply as it does them. That can't-do voice is a dead weight pulling down everyone in their sphere of influence.

C   n e o   tt t   e C   n est e   o   e   to o   se

In 1952, Dr. Norman Vincent Peale wrote a book that became one of the bestselling releases of its time. *The Power of Positive Thinking* addressed, in straightforward language, why attitude is the most important factor in achieving personal happiness. Millions adopted Peale's positive approach to living as part of their lives.

Though it didn't explain it in this fashion, Peale's book is essentially about the way we talk to ourselves. If we are negative, if we spend our lives waiting for something bad to happen, then one of two things will transpire. We will either be confronted by something bad or we will die waiting to have something bad hit us. Neither of these options offers much comfort.

The Dangers of Our Negative Words

Howard Hughes was a genius, a maverick, and a dreamer. His successes in business, aviation, and media made him one of the world's wealthiest and most powerful individuals, but even though he was blessed with incredible riches and was admired by millions, Hughes's attitude doomed him to withdraw from the world.

For decades, hiding behind closed curtains and locked doors, Howard Hughes lived his life in fear, terrified that he was going to get sick and die. Sadly, his fear of death caused him to miss most of the joy of life. His self-concept, the words he spoke to himself, drowned him in a sea of misery. His incredible wealth made his death that much more ironic. Yet though he may have taken it to the extreme, Hughes is just one of millions who tell themselves they have so much to fear that their worries never allow them to fully enjoy a single moment of life.

A Solid Self-View Can Start a Revolution

A good self-concept is vital to making an impact with your words. If you have a positive approach to your life, if you believe in your potential, then others will notice and want to follow you. Even if you don't realize it, you will be a leader.

Throughout the 1930s, Hollywood produced scores of films that featured an underdog overcoming the odds and rising to the top. Nowhere was this more prevalent than in the musicals of the era. In the plot of one musical, an understudy who believed in herself was pushed into the lead part on opening night and proved her worth in front of a theater filled with skeptical patrons. The underlying theme of all of these films, be they musicals or movies about boxers, racehorses, senators, or even John Doe, is that the underdog looked in the mirror and said, "I can do this!"

Hattie McDaniel was an incredibly talented woman who was born a century too early to be fully recognized by her peers. A gifted singer and performer, in the 1930s she turned to acting to pay the rent. With her large figure and expressive face, she was a regular character actress in many of the top films of the decade. Still, the African-American woman seemed doomed to be little more than a background player whose portrayals continued a negative stereotype of her race.

In 1939, Hollywood released what is still considered to be one of the finest films ever made. Based on a bestselling novel, *Gone with the Wind* is four hours of drama, excitement, and history all set in the Old South. The cast assembled for the feature represented a who's who of the industry. As the most-hyped film ever, this was a movie that every A-list actor wanted to be in.

One of the featured parts of this Civil War–era epic was written for a house slave everyone called Mammy. A lot of African-American women auditioned for the role, but the producer, David O. Selznick, sensed that Hattie McDaniel was perfect for the part.

By playing Mammy, McDaniel would make more money in a few months than she had made in all her years of acting. However, it also placed her in the uncomfortable position of playing a slave at the same time African-Americans were beginning to fight to gain equal status. So before signing the contract, Hattie had a talk with herself, then a conversation with the producer. She explained to Selznick that she wanted to play Mammy with dignity, that she wanted this woman to be a three-dimensional character who might be a slave but who still had great strength. Her Mammy would have incredible influence wrapped in an independent spirit. Finally, she wanted the producer to know that she would not say a single line of dialogue that would disparage her race. The risk McDaniel took was huge—she was well aware Selznick could have chosen someone else—but he agreed to her terms. He understood her feelings, and her words drew him to make the changes to accommodate the woman's strong values.

Over the course of the filming, Hattie became one of the favorite members of the cast. The crew loved her, and at a time when race divided everything, she was treated as an equal even to the great Clark Gable. She was anything but a token minority; her attitude made her an equal on the set.

Hattie's portrayal in *Gone with the Wind* reflected her dynamic can-do spirit and transformed Mammy from a background figure to one of the most important characterizations ever to grace a Hollywood film. Because of the way she spoke to herself, and the strength that gave her, when she won an Oscar for her performance, McDaniel made a huge statement for her race as well. The black woman with the can-do attitude paved the way for all the African-American talent that followed in her footsteps.

t's ot t to C ee o se n

Where do you start to change the way you speak to yourself? How do you find the positive words that will lift you up rather than put you down? You can start by making a list.

1. First write down your talents. What do you do well? A good shopper doesn't go to the store without a list, so start to feel good about yourself by putting your talents on paper.

2. What makes you happy? Make a list. This is vital because you won't be positive if you hate the things you do.

3. List your accomplishments. Everyone has accomplished things. They may seem ordinary to you, but they are a part of who you are. By writing them down, you will start to understand what others see as your best traits.

4. Take a look at your strengths and be proud of them. If you emphasize those strengths, the thoughts that hold you back will soon fade, as will many doubts and fears. Remember you can have the skills to do a job, but until you tell yourself you can do it, you will probably fail.

Praise Yourself!

If you are a parent, remember the time your child took his or her initial unsteady steps or said his or her first words. You praised them, bragged on them, hugged them, and made them feel like they were the most special person in the whole world. They were so thrilled by this praise that they tried to take another step or say even more words. Receiving praise was a vital part of their learning.

So when you accomplish something important in your life, even if it's small, you need to do the same thing for yourself. Tell yourself how proud you are of each positive thing you do.

I have known many people who have attempted to lose weight. Most of them would try every diet and start several different exercise programs. Many failed again and again because they went into the venture telling themselves they couldn't do it. Others who had positive attitudes going in but had their minds set only on the big goal failed as well. Their mind was so focused on the big picture that when they accomplished their first very important steps, they didn't stop and praise themselves for losing those first few pounds. Because the long-range goal seemed forever far away, their "self-talk" transformed into negative comments about how they were moving too slowly and they gave up.

No child goes from taking a step to winning gold in the Olympics in a week, and that holds true for adults as well. If Nola Ochs had not praised herself for each of her steps, she certainly never would have made it through her first community-college class, much less become a college graduate working on her master's degree.

The Yardstick Is Your Own

Many people are negative because they measure themselves against others. If you have never run, you are not going to go out your first day and match the times or distances of your neighbor who has jogged for years. Your initial goal needs to be jogging just a few steps one day and then equaling it the next. That is enough to allow yourself to praise your own efforts.

I don't like exercise. To me it seems like work, and I dread it. Yet I find when I simply go into a jog with a positive attitude, wearing a smile on my face, it becomes something I can enjoy. How do I accomplish that? I do it by thinking about my cousin who is suffering with MS and cannot even get out of her wheelchair. She would love to run, so when I consider what a blessing it is that I can run, I find I have more energy than I believed possible. When I change my attitude, the words I speak to myself are changed, and the jog becomes much easier.

Being able to do anything constructive is a joy we overlook, and we need to remind ourselves of that as we start each new task. If we think of each day of life as a blessing, the real joy of being positive begins to take over everything we do. And with that feeling in our hearts, the words that we speak to ourselves, as well as those we speak to others, will be positive as well.

o e n on ent o
os t e t oo

You have heard it all your life, but it's hard to stay positive about anything, including yourself, if you are surrounded by negative people and negative influences. If people are always putting you down, you are probably going to take some of those words to heart. Once you do your inventory and find things that are worth celebrating in your life, you don't need to be around those who revel in their own failures and unhappiness.

So step one in bringing a sense of value and self-worth to your self-communication is to push yourself away from friends who are negative or self-destructive. Some people just love to be miserable. They complain about everything and then blame everyone else for their problems.

They thrive in a world where they are surrounded by others with the same attitude. Even their thoughts are often filled with hate. They simply want to lash out and put others down to give themselves value. That is anything but a positive environment, and no one who wants to make a meaningful impact in the world needs to stay in that situation.

Negative Thoughts Show

People who carry around trash in their heads, people who have low self-esteem, people who are convinced they have little value, show that attitude in the way they look, walk, and talk.

I have a good friend who is just a normal-looking person. He would not be considered handsome, he is not an athlete, and he doesn't have many outstanding talents. Yet he is successful. Why? First, he understands what his strengths are and plays to them. Two, he looks in the mirror and likes who he sees. Three, he is always smiling. The wise man who discovered that happy people attract others discovered one of the keys to a successful life. And finally, no matter who is in a room, no matter their demographic group or social standing, Jim walks in believing he belongs with them. When he comes into a room, everyone seems to notice, and because he is sincerely glad to be there, they are glad to see him.

A Daily Cleanup

A friend once asked me, "Besides your family, who is the most important person in your life?"

I figured my friend was fishing for a compliment, so I said, "My best friend." But that wasn't the right answer.

I thought a bit more and rattled off, "My doctor? My pastor? My lawyer? My editor?" Each of my responses brought a smile and a shake of the head. Finally, after another dozen guesses, I gave up and asked, "Then who?"

"The garbage man," came the simple reply. "Ace Collins, you are the most positive person I know. Nothing keeps you down for long. A blue funk for you lasts just a few minutes. You always find ways to keep on the sunny side. But if the garbage man quit coming to your house, think how it would affect you. As the smell surrounded you, as the trash piled up all over your yard, as the flies and other pests swarmed into your home, you would become more and more unsettled. Things you once ignored would become huge problems. You would start to feel ill, you would lash out at your family and friends with harsh words, and your positive attitude would become harder and harder to maintain. Eventually you would fall under the weight of the trash and grow depressed. Therefore it is the garbage man who is the most important person in your life. He is the one who makes your world a positive one."

I thought about that analogy for a while and realized how inclusive it is. My friend was talking about the garbage on the outside of my world, but there is also the garbage that people carry around inside their head. Their homes may be spotless, but their minds are often filled with all the wrongs that have ever been done to them.

They constantly think about every grudge. They remember every mistake they have made. They continually plot ways to get even with enemies and are forever trying to come to grips with the times they have embarrassed themselves.

A human mind can carry around only so much garbage before that trash starts spewing out in our attitudes toward others and ourselves. The best way to keep a positive attitude is to get rid of your daily trash before you go to sleep each night. You can't help others until you clean out the trash inside yourself. It's not that hard to do either.

1. When you speak to yourself, admit your mistakes and realize that everyone makes them.
2. Work on ridding yourself of the baggage that you see in yourself.
3. Do things that make you happy. You can't change the past, but you can learn from it and move on. Don't let the past fester in your mind. Throw it away!
4. Catch yourself before you say something negative, and try to keep negative thoughts out of your head. Even if you have to make a sign and put it on your wall, embrace and remember the "I think I can" attitude.
5. Hold on to principles that you can be proud of and make them part of your dealings with others. I used to yell at officials at ballgames. Then I realized not only how stupid I looked but how it

affected me. I grew angry, I was unhappy, and I sure wasn't someone I would want to hang around with. When I saw that picture of myself, I realized I needed to change.

6. Seek hobbies that bring you joy and that you can share with others. I fix up old classic cars and drive them because I love the way that seeing these ancient vehicles makes others honk, wave, and smile. So find something that you like that brings positive emotions to others as well.

7. Realize that not everyone will like you or understand you. Will Rogers said he never met a man he didn't like. Will was a positive, upbeat man who considered each day of life such a sweet blessing that he probably did find something to like in everyone. But by the same token, a lot of folks were jealous of his happiness and success. So if someone wrongs you, pray for them, but don't lose sleep over the fact that they don't care for or understand you.

8. Like my friend Jim, look on the sunny side, and you will find a lot of people will be drawn to you. You will also discover that when you talk to yourself, even when you mess up, your words will be understanding, uplifting, and positive.

9. Finally, and probably most important, be yourself. Nola Ochs didn't worry about being out of place on a college campus, and because of her attitude,

she fit in just as well as the other students who were seventy years her junior. In the segregated era, Hattie McDaniel didn't run from her skin color but used it to elevate others by standing proudly at the top of her profession, thus paving the way for a new generation to be given better opportunities. Nola and Hattie liked themselves enough to thrive in worlds few like them would have dared enter. That is the key for each of us. If you are being who you are supposed to be, you will be happy.

Before we can use any of our words to lift anyone else up, we have to use them to elevate our own attitudes. We must have a can-do attitude before we can do anything for ourselves or others. So remember: the first person you need to impact with your words is yourself.

25 Days, 26 Ways to Make This Your Best Christmas Ever

Ace Collins,
Bestselling Author

It's Beginning to Look a Lot Like Christmas

Finding the perfect gift. Maxing out the credit cards—again. Endless baking. Surely there is more to Christmas than this.

Bestselling author Ace Collins wants to help you make this Christmas your best holiday ever! As he blends fascinating stories from history and spiritual truths about the holiday season, he gently guides you toward a new way of thinking about Christmas.

As you explore Collins' twenty-six easy ways to revolutionize your Christmas expectations, you'll feel yourself relax. You'll begin to recapture the joy and magic of the season and to remember the reason we celebrate. Step by step, you'll make small changes in your attitude toward Christmas that will yield big results.

Each upbeat chapter contains easy to apply ideas, from making the most of long lines and traffic jams, to discovering the deeper meaning behind common Christmas symbols. Simple tasks like mailing Christmas cards or holiday shopping that once seemed like dreaded chores will become easier and worthwhile. Collins adeptly shows how to navigate the stressors that threaten to derail the joy of the season. You'll rediscover Christmas as it was meant to be.

Holiday happiness is attainable with this timely and wise book. Reading this partly devotional, partly practical, and always thoughtful book, you are only twenty-five days and twenty-six ways away from your best Christmas ever!

Sticks and Stones

Using Your Words as
a Positive Force

Ace Collins,
Bestselling Author

Of the roughly thirty-thousand
words you will speak today, imag-
ine if just a handful of them could save a life ...

or heal a broken heart ...

or inspire a vision that shapes the course of history.

Today is your opportunity to speak—or write—words
of incalculable potential for good. With simple action
points and colorful stories, this inspiring book will help
you weed out sticks-and-stones negativism and unleash
the surpassing, life-giving, destiny-shaping power of positive words.

What does it take for your words to make a difference? Perhaps a simple thank-you letter. Maybe an encouraging email. Or a simple hello, a thoughtful phone
call, a note written on the back of a family photograph
... the possibilities are endless. *Sticks and Stones* shows
you the power and importance of your words, and how
to use the right words to have a positive impact beyond
anything you can imagine.

Stories Behind Women of Extraordinary Faith

Ace Collins,
Bestselling Author

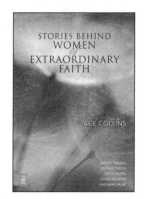

Twenty Women Whose Faith Has Reshaped the World

Ace Collins employs all his storytelling skill to uncover the deeply personal stories of women whose faith shines for us today. Explore twenty different tales of unparalleled inspiration. Learn how each woman's prayers were heard and answered, and discover how each story can light the way on your own journey of faith.

Available in stores and online!

Stories Behind the Traditions and Songs of Easter

Ace Collins,
Bestselling Author

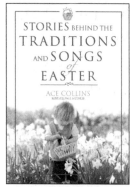

The treasured traditions of Easter—little bunnies, parades, new Easter outfits, sunrise services, passion plays, and more—infuse our celebration of the season with meaning and glowing memories. And in ways you may not realize, they point us to the resurrection of Christ and our hope of life beyond the grave. *Stories Behind the Traditions and Songs of Easter* reveals the events and backgrounds that shaped the best-loved customs and songs of Easter, introducing you to stories you've never heard and a deeper appreciation for the holiday's familiar hallmarks.

Available in stores and online!

Farraday Road

Ace Collins,
Bestselling Author

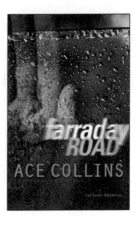

A quiet evening ends in murder on a muddy mountain road.

Local attorney Lije Evans and his beautiful wife, Kaitlyn, are gunned down. But the killers don't expect one of their victims to live. After burying Kaitlyn, Lije is on a mission to find her killer—and solve a mystery that has more twists and turns than an Ozark-mountain back road.

When the trail of evidence goes cold, complicated by the disappearance of the deputy who found Kaitlyn's body at the scene of the crime, Lije is driven to find out why he and his wife were hunted down and left for dead along Farraday Road. He begins his dangerous investigation with no clues and little help from the police. As he struggles to uncover evidence, will he learn the truth before the killers strike again?

Available in stores and online!

Stories Behind the Great Traditions of Christmas

Ace Collins

The cheer of a crackling hearth fire.

Colorful cards from friends and loved ones.

An evergreen tree festooned with ornaments.

The golden traditions of Christmas—gifts, wreaths, stockings, carols, mistletoe, and more—infuse our celebration of the season with meaning and glowing memories. And in ways you may not realize, they point us to the birth of Christ.

Stories Behind the Great Traditions of Christmas reveals the people, places, and events that shaped the best-loved customs of this merriest of holidays. Here are spiritual insights, true-life tales, and captivating legends to intrigue you and your family and bring new luster and depth to your celebration of Jesus' birth. Discover how

- after eighteen centuries of all but ignoring the event, churches began to open the door for believers to commemorate Jesus' incarnation.
- the evergreen tree, once a central theme in the worship practices of pagan cultures, came to represent the everlasting love of God.
- the magi's three gifts—gold, frankincense, and myrrh—are filled with spiritual symbolism.

The traditions of Christmas lend beauty, awe, and hope to the holiday, causing people all over the world to anticipate it with joy. The stories in this book will warm your heart as you rediscover the true and eternal significance of Christmas.

Share Your Thoughts

With the Author: Your comments will be forwarded to the author when you send them to *zauthor@zondervan.com*.

With Zondervan: Submit your review of this book by writing to *zreview@zondervan.com*.

Free Online Resources at
www.zondervan.com

Zondervan AuthorTracker: Be notified whenever your favorite authors publish new books, go on tour, or post an update about what's happening in their lives at www.zondervan.com/authortracker.

Daily Bible Verses and Devotions: Enrich your life with daily Bible verses or devotions that help you start every morning focused on God. Visit www.zondervan.com/newsletters.

Free Email Publications: Sign up for newsletters on Christian living, academic resources, church ministry, fiction, children's resources, and more. Visit www.zondervan.com/newsletters.

Zondervan Bible Search: Find and compare Bible passages in a variety of translations at www.zondervanbiblesearch.com.

Other Benefits: Register yourself to receive online benefits like coupons and special offers, or to participate in research.

ZONDERVAN®

ZONDERVAN.com/
AUTHORTRACKER
follow your favorite authors